FRAMING THE DARK

FRAMING THE DARK

Dread By Design in Motion Pictures

By David Aldrich

Dal LaMagna Publishing, 2009

REEL U FILMS

ISBN 978-0-9821863-0-5
© 2009 by David Aldrich
All rights reserved
First Edition

The movies made me do it. Must have made for some fixation on frightful things. My mother told me that my first peek at the screen was in the middle of the picture. She got the usher to let us in for just a minute, time for her toddler to take in that amazing sight. Some poor man lashed to a mast was getting a good flogging. Undoubtedly scarred for good and traumatized, I can't remember it at all.

I do remember what followed:

At the tender age of six being taken down ***The Spiral Staircase,*** and all the way down in darkness having the daylights scared out of me. Then no longer safe at home when required to go to the basement. My older brother was sometimes there, waiting for me in shadow.

And just one year later with ***Great Expectations*** I was on the moor at night, running with some boy alone, taken there by the shudder of its setting and shock of its surprise. I still see that bent tree reaching for me in that empty expanse of creeping fog and gasping wind. I was stunned by a shocking appearance, and, for the first time, struck by the wonder of photography and film.

And around that time abandoned at ***Snow White.*** My brother's friend, a big fifth-grader, couldn't take it anymore and was becoming quite distracting, so our mother hauled the shrieking boy outside, well out of earshot. I suppose she didn't want the spell broken for her little ones left behind or for the wicked witch and that specter in the mirror.

Now, I'm not one to blame my parents for everything, but there still is no good reason for a family outing to end up at the Bates Motel. And before we could recover back home, my father, with a look unbecoming his proper upbringing, plopped a mop on his head, grabbed a butcher knife, and coming up from behind us, completely freaked my brother out—evening one score.

There were more before, and many more after, and I was doing it on my own. It didn't matter anymore. Long ago it already was too late.

Enabling me to follow my fixation here, I have my close friends to thank: my brother Jonathan (teacher and poet) for the main title and sharp eye for dull wording, and more; Lonnie Duka (photographer and filmmaker) for the covers and centerpiece, and his good thoughts in between; Dal LaMagna (film producer and Tweezerman) for getting everything to come together in a good way; Peter O'Malley (too many expertises to cull down) for early re-views and valued encouragement; and my wonderful wife, Kim, for putting up with much too much time spent dealing with all the demons.

For my parents, Bailey and Elizabeth Perkins Aldrich

—D. A.

Contents

Introduction: The Horrific Chiller

We know it when we see it. We recognize the film's imagery, feel the familiar dread of its suspense, and even foresee what we are in for. We know the horrific chiller by the shape of our sensations, yet are surprisingly unable to describe it in any other form. By definition, all of these films evoke powerful emotions unique to the genre, but the shared qualities within the pictures that cause our unshakable reactions are evasive. We might recall alien beings or supernatural forces, but we also remember terribly disturbing chillers that were entirely naturalistic. We might think of primitive violence, but there are some unusually frightening films that are completely lacking any depicted brutality. There is a remarkable range of films evoking such a singular response. What is it that we see when enveloped by deep and dark disturbance?

Wondering what unites these differing stories with shared experience, I could not complete the answer. Certainly all the films center on primitive conflict, and their characters confront extended peril and possible destruction. True and inclusive, but not very useful, the observation equally applies to other melodramas, films that take us to the edge of our seats, but no farther. Action adventure movies, missions of mortal combat, progress from mounting danger to life-threatening assaults, yet spare us the worst disturbance. Suspense lacks the chiller's unsettling sense of unnatural dread, and the climax is free of horror and lasting impact. There is even less distress from disaster pictures. Although they feature destruction taking countless victims, we enjoy the spectacle while avoiding the holocaust. I could not grasp what ingredients were missing from all these nonhorrific melodramas, the elusive elements seen in every memorable chiller, and my look through film books failed to disclose them.

Seeking what should be obvious, undoubtedly a short and simple answer, an afternoon's exercise turned into a lengthy endeavor. The puzzle's hard-to-get solution did turn out to be simple, but its complexities suggested that I had just started. In a sure step-by-step course a journey unfolded, one that took me in unforeseen and previously rejected directions.

Systematic analysis was certain to uncover common ingredients, but the telling nature of what was discovered came as a complete surprise. Shared elements pieced together into a singular picture of startling clarity, simplicity, and completeness, and every element explained itself by being a proven trigger of automatic emotion. The message was revealed and its codes of communication broken.

The surprising scope of a short formula left so little unsaid that I felt it was possible to complete the picture. Moving on to the fabric of frightening scenes, then to whole films, and finally through all the arts and crafts, the search found not only what we always see, but how films are best fashioned to make us feel the way we do.

I. Finding the Formula

The horrific chiller is defined by feelings inside of us rather than by features within the films, and it is difficult to identify what is seen that makes these shows unique. Possibly there are no universals. Few art forms are always essentially the same, and chillers might tap a variety of unrelated anxieties and do so by differing designs. It is also possible, however, that they all enact various versions of the same story and employ a fixed formula. This proves to be the case. A search for uniformities uncovers common ingredients of shared imagery and events. Present in every effective example of the genre, never all together in other motion pictures, they provide a true generic description, the origin of our emotion.

Distilling the Elements

We know these movies by sensations. Suspense is infused with an insidious sense of morbid dread, shock is more profound than a reflexive reaction to the grotesque or unexpected, and terror does not end with the movie, but continues to resonate its dark disturbance. Films most consistently evoking these defining emotions for more than one generation of viewers were selected for study, and they included examples from every conceivable category.

The search began by looking at everything. Anything anywhere that appeared to create tension was listed, as well as every ingredient within frightening scenes. All of these listings were described by their many attributes, from specific features to abstract qualities. Somewhere within this vast collection would be the dimensions of common ground.

As anticipated, only a few attributes were found in every film, and some of these appeared in most dramas that include danger. A small number remained, however, and they were all refined to best describe what is always seen in the wide array of individual examples.

Suddenly all the elements clustered and crystallized into clear shapes, and they created a split picture. Victims are reshaped by two forms of assault, and the agent's imagery sends sensations of both experiences. Similar to a particularly pleasing mathematical solution, the formula displayed unusual simplicity, symmetry, and sweep of explanation. All of its elements appear in all the films, and they include all of the frightening ingredients. Together they prove to be the whole picture in a singular formula. Properly presented in poorly made movies, they can provide the complete experience. Without them, even well-crafted, violent dramas fail to be deeply disturbing.

The Generic Form

Horrific chillers that deliver everything are assemblies of the same elements. The most compact description of the genre is followed by definitions of the elements. When experiencing deepening dread and haunting shock, we are always witnessing *dissolution of selfhood and its primal extinction by an obsessive and totalistic humanlike being that embodies both assaults.*

Selfhood (personal identity, the ability to be ourselves): We may see a wide variety of circumstances and surroundings, but something central to our sense of self will always be disappearing. We could be in our home alone at night, snugly under covers, close to slumber, before the bursting wide of our bedroom door. And before the swing of blade that takes our face, finding ourselves overcome as easily as the shield around our safest space was shattered, we are overtaken by the terrible sense that there is no self safe and separate from outside forces.

A horrific situation could be science fiction, a close encounter of the worst kind, one that dissolves our willpower and leaves us forced to do their bidding. It could also be something far less fantastic, no more than a strange and unsettling setting that denies our basic ability to act and understand—but there will always be an assault upon the essence of ourselves.

The loss of individual self is a fate worse than death. We see some poor soul taken from his cage for a fiendish operation. Should he emerge transformed, personality replaced and appearance wholly altered, though he is now feeling fine, not too bright but blissfully unaware of an identity that no longer has any meaning, we are likely to feel it would be nicer not to survive the procedure. Even excruciating scenes of torture become ghastly only when centering on our sense of self. The horror is from being so unnaturally immobilized, so stripped of self and self-protection, unable to move even while they have their way with us, and the feeling of our own erasure will be heightened by any stripping of personal appearance. At the movies, if not elsewhere, the most terrible fright proves more connected to selfhood than to life and limb.

Picture this. Behind the back wall, deep down in the basement, there is that sound again. Barely audible, but definitely there, and this time it seems to be something of some size and moving along the wall. Stepping to its new location, we put our ear to the wall, old discolored fiberboard with stains that streak from above. All is still, and after some waiting we rap twice. Hearing no response, we give the board a solid slap, but there is barely any sound at all as our hand passes through the startlingly soft and soggy paneling. More falls away with our withdrawn hand, revealing an unknown room. Collecting ourselves and grabbing a flashlight, we easily enlarge an entrance and see no signs of any presence. Entering, it is all darkness with a beam of light that ends on a stone wall with mold and slimy moss, and we are instantly overtaken by a damp chill and dank smell. A few more cautious steps and a drop of liquid falls on our outstretched hand with flashlight. We look up and another drop strikes our eye. We are also having trouble with our footing. Instinctively attempting a wide stride, we find ourselves unnaturally slowed. Light downward reveals an earthen floor, soft in some places, wet all over. We hop to another place, but our feet sink deeper, and it takes a few more steps to free ourselves. The spot of light slowly passing across boggy ground continues to find nothing else until finally falling on a sunken line, maybe six inches wide, running along the paneled wall. Searching for something more, we find indications of another trough, then a smooth, continuous trail. The sharp edge of illumination travels along the shallow path, then freezes where it ends—a dark hole, a bit bigger than your fist.

Seeing this at the movies should be more disturbing than another show, one in which a soldier tries to make his way safely through a minefield. Although danger may be lacking in the basement, suddenly finding ourselves inside some soft and slimy world—having the sense of being absorbed and possibly headed for something worse—each careful step now taken there will be fraught with a far more dreadful form of fear.

Suspense in a more everyday melodrama comes with the approach of a tangible threat, but high anxiety in the chiller has a more discomposing nature, and it may arise with no imminent danger in sight. There is something seen in the character on-screen: the feeling of impotence, lost control and understandings, and that awful sense of removal while being enveloped by a malignant environment. The foundations of selfhood, a separate existence without isolation, and connectedness without lost control, are in jeopardy. It is always this way in the most terrible times. Just as the worst conclusion is the taking of self, the most frightful start is the very visceral sensation of its erosion.

dissolution (dissolving of self, its definition and boundaries, lost ability to act and understand): All horrific chillers portray a world of no sanctuary, especially within ourselves. In many of the classics we need only sense something amiss to know this discomfort. When a menace does take shape, our uneasiness becomes the sensation of being helplessly overpowered. Related feelings come in other dramas, but we are not simply outgunned in the chiller. Here we are at a loss by being drained of normal power, and this helplessness is far more dreadful. Seeing a killer in a car pursue a running victim meets the requirements of melodrama, but not necessarily of chiller. Give the victim the vehicle, and show him, overrushed by high anxiety, flood the engine and then completely lose all composure. We may have seen it all before, but it still is much more unsettling.

All horrific chillers strip us of our normal modes of action or reason, a peeling away of ourselves that leaves us crippled and wide open. Sometimes, especially when confronting surreal powers, personal boundaries will literally dissolve and we experience the unnatural invasion of external forces. In all instances, our boundaries are dangerously altered. In a wide variety of thrillers, many memorable scenes take place in the most crowded, common, and benign locations where we suddenly feel isolated, abandoned, and nakedly exposed. This is also the feeling in the other most disturbing location, intimate places, such as bedroom or bath. These big and small spots, ordinarily free even of the thought of intrusion, will prove terrifying when failing to provide protection. If we were to see Alfred Hitchcock's classic shower sequence unaltered (***Psycho***, U.S.A., 1960) but preceded by the intruder forcing the woman into the bathroom instead of suddenly appearing through the misty curtain, even the masterful montage that follows would lose notable impact. It is not simply that the assault takes place in the shower. Through the veil that separates us from the outside world, our most intimate space has been invaded.

primal extinction (savage or elemental demolishment): After our sense of self starts to erode, we face selfhood's primal annihilation. Once Hitchcock's psychopath has violated private boundaries, we confront extinction in its purest form. Although the victim has been the film's central character, we respond less to her death than to the primitive mutilation of person, and without actually seeing her stabbed, we complete the picture of frenzied demolition. We do see her collapse, tearing down the thin curtain that has failed to shield her, and we witness what was part of her drain away and disappear forever. Typical of many classic scenes of totalistic extinction, the disappearance is primal in two respects: bestial (ferocious disfigurement or consumption) and elemental (absorption, draining, melting, transformation, or erasure). One or both forms will always arrive in the vanishing of personal presence. The risk of being shot, so high in most dramas of murder and mayhem, is near zero here. Bullets don't cut it. Our concerns have little connection to bodily harm, and everything to do with saving our skin.

the being: More surprising than all chillers sending the same message is that it is always delivered by such a singular agent. Our identity is threatened by some entity that, despite its diverse forms, exhibits an unusual number of shared characteristics. Many serve no practical purpose in the story. None are required to execute a similar threat, and some may be so unlikely that they have to be explained away. Often independent of each other in nature, yet always all here, their collective reappearances must have universal meaning. The menace reveals itself to be the message, and it can be delivered at a distance—an assault felt deep inside of us, even from a far-off sighting.

obsessive and totalistic (unyielding desire, lacking other dimensions): Obsession begins with intent, and that alone may make peril horrific. A lesser danger that expresses intent can be more awesome than impending disaster. We see someone on a barren expanse of land that suddenly develops widening and rapidly elongating cracks. Should these fractures dart toward him no matter which way he runs, it could be no more than bad luck, but the suggestion of some inexplicable purpose provides the potential for horror. But for the lack of intent, the circumstances are similar in **Earthquake** (U.S.A., 1974) and far worse, and this absence renders even more certain catastrophes less terrible.

Obsession is also relentless. The leaden, unrelenting gait of the living dead stamps a powerful imprint of its aim on us. Although the slow motion should work to our advantage, we see something inescapable. By gait or by behavior, unusual determination will always be communicated, and our reaction will be beyond reason. Even a large number of people out to get us will be less disconcerting than the dogged pursuit of one driven individual.

Obsession in chillers is totalistic, unnaturally stripping its agent of other concerns. Not all horrific menaces bear personal animosity or have any desire to see us suffer, but their comforting lack of ill will comes with a blind indifference to everything about us. We become the individual target of oddly impersonal negation, no more than random victims of some unnatural appetite, or innocently in the way of another desire. Beyond obsession nothing matters, surely not us or even what we do to defend ourselves. We are nothing, do not count, and we feel this nullification deep within ourselves well before it comes to pass on-screen.

Suspense and terror may have many sources. A successful nonhorrific thriller can entwine a variety of enemies, motives, and situations, but this is another picture. In horror films there is always that singular agent or identical others, unyielding and single-minded. And when it finds us, every encounter will be a display of obsession. The methodical manner of stalking, even an unleashed and frenzied assault, is performed in a rigid, mechanical fashion. Violence may come without anger, and rage will be confined to a repetitive act with no motion or emotion beyond its malignant purpose. We see sure signs of ritualized compulsion, and the sight is instantly chilling. Our alarm is greatly exaggerated, and it is colored by the more unsettling sensation of unnatural dread.

The appearance of obsession may bring terror to mere melodrama, and it makes horror more dreadful. Defined by its subject matter, **Marathon Man** (U.S.A., 1976) is a conventional conspiratorial thriller. Political and criminal intrigue provides the entanglement, and multiple plot lines and themes are followed. It is also a superbly crafted, shocking chiller with periods of horrific fright. In its best-remembered scene, Dustin Hoffman has been snatched from the sanctuary of his bath and finds himself powerless in an alien place, strapped in a dentist's chair with Laurence Olivier employing painful dental surgery to extract information. Hoffman has no idea why he is there, what his abductors want, or even the meaning of a repeatedly asked question. This taking of self, made inert and unknowing, could hardly be more horrific, but the old man's manner carries additional chemistry. Olivier is a refined, elderly gentleman who reacts with professional concern about overlooked decay found in Hoffman's mouth while going about his business of applied suffering. There is no trace of sadistic pleasure in this tired old man, only that terrible detachment from cruelty. He is even removed from the fact that his question is meaningless to his would-be informer, and it makes the single-minded obsession absolute. Hoffman confronts what will be found in all horrific obsessions. He cannot reason with it or trade on feelings. It is irrevocable. For horrific beings, beyond the measure of mere obsession, the desire will be totalistic. The creature comes with no unnecessary interests or abilities, and every one of its salient features advances or announces the mission.

humanlike (more and less than human): Horror shows have their roots in the embryonic development of moving pictures. When films began to assume narrative form, the fantasy film became one of the first movie genres. Although these science-fiction adventures were not chillers, they did introduce moments of fright. The shock premise rarely changed. An Arctic explorer suddenly gobbled up by an abominable snow giant is typical (**The Conquest of the Pole**, France, 1912), an unforeseen and brief encounter with the jaws of a humanlike monster. It was not long before gothic literature was found to be supremely suited to visual presentation, and the horror film was born.

Once again the threat was embodied in a being, but now it was far more human in appearance. It is the focus of virtually every old silent and talking chiller, and memorably so in the classics: a mindless, ashen-skinned somnambulist (**The Cabinet of Dr. Caligari**, Germany, 1919); a rat-faced vampire (**Nosferatu**, Germany, 1921); a skull-faced madman (**The Phantom of the Opera**, U.S.A., 1925); a batlike vampire (**Dracula**,

U.S.A., 1931); an oversize, composite living corpse (**Frankenstein**, U.S.A., 1931). It remained this way for films that soon followed and remains this way today. The most dreadfully disturbing films will always feature a most singular danger, an entity alive with desires displaying the same designs.

Back inside that hidden basement room, working up the nerve to inspect that hole, we carefully make our way across soft ground, then crouch and train the light on the open spot. An explosive hiss and burst of head send us backward, a stunning blur of something instantly gone back within its tunnel. Now we can see it well. A cylindrical body with flattened face is all pasty, translucent flesh with a network of bluish veins deep inside. Large jelly eyes lacking any pupil become obscured by the wide-open, whiskered catfish mouth, pulsating with deep bursts of breath.

embodies both assaults (physically reflects personal dissolution and selfhood's primal extinction): The agent of our twin fates mirrors both of them in its appearance. A vacant void of missing person and the threat of primitive annihilation are features of virtually every menace that assumes horrific proportions. The psychotic slasher is all that and no more. This cliché killer of the shock genre is recognized by two signatures that completely define its fearsome identity: aberrant face and tightly gripped, oversize knife. The facial disfigurement may be inborn or by accident, slight or extreme, but the signs are clear. There is something amiss in the eyes and about the mouth, freezing them in a cold leer. This comes with a general loss of facial features, smoothed or melted, and the overall specter provides a definite sense of eroded self and lost humanity. The slasher's second signal, its primitive weapon, is ever present, not concealed before striking or left at the scene of the crime. Clutched with arm extended and reflexively employed in a fixed manner, the blade might just as well be part of the body. Much like an animal displaying threatening tooth and claw, it embodies the other side of the horrific experience, primal extinction.

The cliché killer rarely possesses any other significant physical attributes, save possibly a large size or an obsessive feature such as a slowed step. There need be no more. Dissolution and primal destruction say it all, and they will be there regardless of circumstances. If lacking the facial signatures, the man is likely to disguise himself with a mask that presents the missing signs, hiding who he is, but not what. As seen throughout the chiller's evolution, it will be a slit-eyed grimace and malignant human features void of person. In the surprisingly smart and scary slaughter film **Scream** (U.S.A., 1996), by employing a white mask of death, warped and wobbly, as if reflected in a fun house mirror, director Wes Craven gives a nice new twist to the old design. Dark cutout cavities of eyes and mouth with wavy outlines are elongated, stretching downward rather than across the face. Its distinctive perversity is discomposing, reminiscent of Munch's primal scream of a pulled-apart soul.

The slasher's mask has remarkable dimensions. It is a symbol that simultaneously exists as three opposites: a mask of identity (conceals self); a revelation of identity (discloses its state of being and purpose); and a mirror of identity (reflects the onlooker's felt dissolution and extinction). In real life, one would have more reason to fear someone who did not announce his purpose or was not limited to a single means of assault. Surely, in film it would be less tiresomely familiar. It takes time and ingenuity, however, to make a murderer of normal appearance more than a minor menace, while the cliché killer is instantly surrounded by an aura of dread. It is powerful testimony to these visual attributes. Overworked in tired formula films, they still continue to evoke true terror. Not confined to instantly identified maniacs and monsters, these expressions of dissolution and primal aggression will be displayed by any danger that becomes the focus of unusual fear, including more ordinary-appearing people, animals, nonliving objects, and forces of nature. Just as the sight of victims disappearing will be seen in two stages, the view of our destroyer will be a stunning preview of both departures.

Applied to any frightening movie, the formula proved true. Films of chilling dread and horrific shock must be more than murder and fights for physical survival, and it will be a show of selfhood's dissolution and primal extinction in both victims and their agents of destruction. Precisely so in the most unsettling films, the picture couldn't be clearer—unmistakable, pure, and perfect portraits of personal disintegration. Unique and universal to the genre, the sought-for elemental definition was revealed, and the inquiry would have ended had its conclusions not proved the start of an unexpected turn.

II. About Face

Seeking only sure ingredients meant steering clear of speculation, and this excluded any thought of finding psychic meanings. Most psychological interpretations of drama and imagery are inherently uncertain, and even truisms should be suspect. Omitting guesswork from the study, however, unexpectedly led to a look inside our mind free of the usual conjecture. Danger's portrait proves to be a composite of pictures with proven meanings. All important features, especially those within its many faces, are symbols of nonverbal expression. We will always see the same two statements clearly spelled out—messages written in three languages of automatic emotion. Still proceeding with certainty, the search shifted to ourselves as the face of terror was confronted head-on.

Images of Genetic Origin

Frightening faces have features more primal than personal experience, and they reveal roots in our distant heritage. Animals, for the most part, are born educated, instinctively reacting with appropriate behavior. Visual signals dominate in the higher animals, and the back-and-forth behavior of social interaction is set by surprisingly simple patterns of stimuli. Birds, for instance, will not feed their young unless their young are begging, and the babies will not beg without being given the right sign. If a herring gull returns to the nest with the red spot on its bill painted out, the chicks will not peck at the beak and will be left unfed. If the adult is replaced with a flat, profile cutout of only the head, marked with the spot and two other features, the babies will go for it, pecking for food. Parental birds do no better, most looking for an open beak and not much more. It could belong to a larger species hatched in the nest, or be no more than a man-made contraption, but the biggest cavity demands the most feeding. These visual cues, known as sign stimuli, are necessary to release a fixed pattern of instinctive behavior. They are also all that is relevant. Remove everything else, and the response is unchanged. Strengthen the stimuli, and reactions are unusually strong.

Human behavior at birth is wired with related designs, and adults are never as free from instinct as they would believe. Before the benefit of any learning, infants respond to features of the human face. Long after matured intellect claims to have replaced primitive mechanisms, we respond to a baby in the same terms, a reflexive reaction to genetically encoded imagery. The sight of an oversize head with large eyes and pug nose activates nurturing and protective instincts. These sign stimuli are exhibited by all human babies, and they are exaggerated in all young animals that silently call for a cuddle, as well as endearing dolls, lovable stuffed creatures, and even E.T. And if after receiving an infant's smile or some sound of distress we find ourselves replying in baby talk, the singsong of sweeping pitches and stressed vowel sounds, we are unwittingly making the very music that their young brains are particularly well tuned to make note of.

We share many expressions with other animals, and most signs of assault will not be subtle or have to be learned. The angled eyes and drawn-back lips exposing prominent teeth are universally associated with aggression in primates as well as other mammals, and they are accompanied by a body posture appearing throughout the animal kingdom. Signs of strength and disposition are recognized everywhere with meanings implanted in all of us.

Threatening designs are so ingrained that they may be felt in film even from nonliving objects without any evidence of danger. In the offbeat comedy *Slither* (U.S.A., 1973), we repeatedly see the same black van coming down the highway well behind the vehicle occupied by our friends. Each time it is seen through a telescopic lens that, while enlarging everything within its narrowed viewpoint, makes distant objects unnaturally inflated compared with a closer foreground. The long lens also flattens perspective, and anything coming our way is oddly slowed in its advancement. Well before the movie provides more than comedy, there is something unsettling about the sight of the van that suggests dire consequences to come. Seen coming up over a rise on the hilly road, expanded in size and flattened in depth, running at speed while barely creeping toward us, the ominously magnified dark mass assumes a disturbing sense of relentlessness, signals so strong that they are experienced on their own with no need for threatening context. When the object is more potentially dangerous, its impact may make us recoil. Shot with the same long lens, a helicopter rising unexpectedly from below our horizontal line of sight is surprisingly alarming even without sound. Floating just above cliffside, looming unusually large while facing us dead-on, it may assume the predatory aura of a gigantic insect. Should it be enormous without the aid of forced perspective, such as an airship or alien craft, we may be overcome. From *War of the Worlds* (U.S.A., 1953) to recent releases, the effect is formidable. Even far away, hovering on a distant horizon, big saucers are remarkably disturbing. Viewed from below, dwarfing skyscrapers and eclipsing the sky, they are awesomely alarming.

Seen across a flat plane, swollen and arising, the opposition says that we won't be competing on a level playing field. Embodiments need not be huge, merely larger than normal. Puffed up and risen above their target is the instinctive pose of dominance creating instant submission from members of the same species and flight from powerful enemies. True to all sign stimuli, when signals are enormous, so is our response. Exaggerated by all slashers, they are also seen to some degree in every fearsome menace. The vision of victims is consistent. Rarely struck from below, never from directly overhead, we usually find ourselves looking up at an angle from a submissive posture, frozen in that awful realization that neither resistance nor submission will save us.

Warnings of Unnatural Attack

Expressions we share with our animal ancestors are part of an innate vocabulary set to trigger one of a few fixed responses. Related languages exist in all social animals, and they regulate interaction, including aggression. Normal animal aggression is without personal malice. Created by competition over such basic needs as food, sex, status, and territory, hostility will be quickly communicated while its consequences remain tightly policed. Weapons raised, cocked and ready, evolved everywhere to avoid their use. Alarming sign stimuli invite conflict that is usually soon settled in the court of expressions and postures. If a fight becomes physical between members of the same species, it may be painful, but it will still remain a choreographed bout with instinctively enforced Queensbury rules.

There is a critical difference between what we see in nature and what is shown at the movies. Even the fiercest attack of one wolf upon another will stop when the loser lies down and exposes its neck in submission, and all menacing expressions soon vanish. In the chiller, however, even if the enemy is one of us, this look is an inborn feature, a frozen assurance of imminent assault persisting regardless of any sign we give or act performed. We are chilled by a horrific alteration of instinctual expressions, the knowledge of its unrelenting obsession with deadly assault as well as our unshakable sense that we are helpless to halt it.

The signals are unnatural in another respect. We not only can't stop it, we did nothing to start it. This variation announces that we are irrelevant, that the target is not our behavior, but our very existence. Our response to such an unnatural message cuts to the core of these movies, revealing a common distinction between the plots of chillers and mere melodrama. Both enact mortal conflicts, but horrific confrontation is usually void of competition. We all recall pictures of unusual suspense and surprise where life-threatening pursuits left us more breathless than lastingly shaken. Reviewing their theme, we are likely to find that the victim is a direct threat to the enemy's goals. Intentionally or not, he has trespassed upon the aggressor's territory. Lacking competition, confrontation here is a most irregular state of affairs, existing simply because we do. If there is any profit in our loss, such as becoming food for a hungry predator, more than any mere meal, we sense being the object of desire to see us gone. Well before contact we are told a terrible tale. Nature arms us with abilities to read and respond to normal encounters, but we are disarmed and disabled by such an aberrant message.

Although we take it for granted that carvings and drawings remain motionless, primitive totems or renderings of humanlike monsters agape with teeth may be more horrific due to their static nature. In film, the pictures do move, and we are quite conscious of our discomfort with the frozen expression on an animate being. This pursuit by a fixed snarl paints a remarkably complete picture of our horrific circumstances. Unchangeable, unflinching even when hurt, this predator never wears out or shifts to an easier selection. Its obsession with us is without provocation, and it conveys less concern with our actions than our personal annihilation. Our fear is equally unrelenting, emotions from inborn signals with unshakable reactions.

Expressions of Aberrant Emotions

Despite all that we learn from jaws ever ready to attack, we sense even more from their peculiar grimace. Lips pulled back from threatening teeth surely form a snarl, but they likely shape a twisted smile as well. Learned meanings for facial expressions horrifically enrich those instinctively known; the introduction of human qualities instilling that awful sense of evil. Heightened capacity for thought and emotion may elevate us from the beast, but when bent toward nihilistic ends it provides passions and possibilities denied to the fiercest of animals. The hate-filled smile is more than threatening. Its contemptuous pleasure is a perverse expression of normally contra-dictory emotions. Similar to the fixed snarl, it is a violent aberration of nature. Together these malignant signals of man and beast reveal a hybrid with more than the worst of both worlds. Animal rage loose from natural restraints is servicing human emotions and intellect void of all humanity. By a small number of facial cues, by a process that does not require our conscious awareness, we clearly behold the visage of absolute evil.

The leer is suggested in virtually every fearful face, whether extreme or slight. It is obvious in many, and odious in the most horrific fiends, often following the snarl. No screen presence better exhibits these two expressions than Lon Chaney's **The Phantom of the Opera,** and no face surpasses his creation for pure visual terror.

Chaney was a master artist of makeup and a consummate mime of expressive behavior. He brought both gifts to silent pictures with a greater understanding of horror than any other performer. His phantom's face is a living skull with two featured expressions. Even when relaxed, withdrawn lips display threatening teeth made more menacing by their uneven shape and separation from each other. When his lips tighten further, the mouth becomes more human in a hideous leer. Expressions of man and animal are also well reflected in his behavior and will be powerfully communicated as the fiend is about to meet his own demise. They are, in fact, his two final statements to the world.

We are underground in the sewers of Paris. Pursued by a mob seeking to destroy him, the phantom finds escape blocked by a dead end. Suddenly spinning to face the enemy, and turning into a wild monkey, he rears upward, arms aloft with fingers curled to grab, and jaws widened in a defiant display of bestial rage. It works, if just for a moment, and the crowd recoils, aghast. Although hopelessly outnumbered, the phantom sees that he still holds the power to strike fear in our hearts, and his animalistic snarl becomes grotesquely twisted into a triumphant human expression of mocking disdain. With contempt he stands his final ground and is done.

Features of Symbolic Design

The horrific menace exhibits a third set of features from a nonverbal language, one neither inherited nor learned from social interaction. Invented anew by every one of us, it is the visual vocabulary of symbolic thought. Although the imagery of our imagination is personally constructed, some is universal. Shared human experience and a common cortex give birth to strikingly similar conceptions. Numerous fearsome features appear in artistic renderings throughout history as well as within our earliest nightmares. They are also found in all memorable film monsters and, to some extent, in every chilling assailant. From the first fantasy film's man-eating giant to present-day creations, prominent teeth remain a common ingredient. We are easily weakened by a winning smile, and by the snarl of a winner as well, and in both cases we are also taken by the teeth.

Though they may be naturalistic (*Jaws*, U.S.A., 1975), teeth easily assume surreal auras distinct from possible pain or injury. To the inborn image of alarm we attach even deeper fears. Sharp and shiny shredders surrounding a dark cavity, all set to cut and swallow, create the perfect combined picture of dissolution and consumption. This primitive design, so pure and simple, becomes the most elemental archetype of our two most feared final stages, and it carries feelings of our completion. When some sinister figure exposes animalistic teeth, more than any concern with bodily harm, we may sense an unnatural unease that someway our selfhood could be stripped away. Symbolic features are also free to mutate. Placed in the hands of a horrific killer, the tooth may become an elongated canine-shaped instrument, driven downward and oddly limited to the slashing movement of devouring jaws. It takes the position of primate claw but, significantly, not its curved design. This is a displaced tooth, maintaining its form and psychic function.

Threatening features need not be fashioned from actual danger. They may be based solely on symbolic significance. We see a man walking, taking the same route of someone some distance ahead of him. Add a clubfoot, deadening his stride as it is dragged forward, and should he have his eyes on the person in front, we may experience a sense of sinister stalking. A physical arrangement for potential alarm becomes a threat because it contains a psychic symbol, and the now confirmed symbol sends its signature impression of relentless pursuit. The man may also be given an unusually vacant face, and we are warned of his disturbing lack of humanity. Should the plot allow for less realism, these dimensions could assume full force. The limp might become the lumbering mechanical gait of the living dead, making obsession certain. The face could be the featureless void of an alien invader, its absence of sentiment absolute. Symbolic features are much more than movie-making conventions with learned meanings. They speak to us personally with wired emotion.

Faces of Identity, Specters of Negation

By our face we are best distinguished from all other forms of life as well as from every other human being. It is the shared sign of our common identity, and it is our most personal signature. With it we present our public persona to the world and conceal our inner self, yet through it we may unwittingly reveal ourselves more truthfully than in words. More than any other external feature, the face is us. When imagined as part of some horrific creature, the visage is likely to tell everything, and even any emptiness will be full of meaning.

Asymmetry is often evident in frightening faces, and in disturbing bodies as well. Disconcerting even to infants, the anomaly will come to be seen by our psyche as malformations and misalignments of the individual's nature. Any alteration of normality assumes significance, and some create unusual anxiety. Looking at what was once a familiar face molded and melted by a tight sheer stocking is troublesome in two respects. Even with the aid of cool intellect, our brain has surprising difficulty with seeing things the way they were. Born able to measure minuscule differences in normal faces, we find such extremes beyond the scope of instinctive computation. Moreover, we find it peculiarly difficult to respond in a cool manner. The situation may be free of fear, but there is something oddly disturbing in the appearance, and without doubt it carries some psychic meaning. All forms of extreme disfigurement provoke strong emotions, but not the eerie sense of dread we receive from a formless void. We see neither an injured human nor a grotesque alien, but a dissolution of the being. Seen in others, it is an awesome display of empty humanity and nonindividuality. Viewed as us in a supernatural film, it is a horrific enactment of our disappearance.

The deathlike look of lost features is often stated as the source of disturbance. Surely our natural fear of death is a more direct explanation than something else it might symbolize. The truth is, however, that even death derives its fearsome image less from its actual condition than from its symbolic nature. In everyday life, the sight of someone either just deceased or in their final skeletal state need not be the slightest bit frightening. Viewed in the process of decay, however, no matter what the context, it is certain to be unsettling. This ultimate expression of an eroded identity is displayed in most envisionings of the grim reaper. Although representing death, it is a being in transition. Decomposed to the point devoid of individuality, residual features remain as powerful reminders of what once was. We see not lack of life, but dissolution and annihilation of selfhood. The face of death, whether real or imagined, is truly horrific only by being the specter of disintegration.

Faces of identity reveal symbolic language separate from facial expressions socially learned or genetically known. The unconscious mind is a magical realm of illusion, allusion, and metaphor where invented symbols become physical realities. The face, so laden with emotional import to our personal self and sense of others, assumes unusual psychic significance. Its design is seen as a complete show of the inside, and even the lack of features, including the manner of their disappearance, tells the bearer's true identity. Threatening specters of negation, whether in a state of decay and dissolution or emptied and annihilated, advertise everything.

Written on the Face (a review)

There is a widespread belief among the public, shared by some members of the advertising industry, that subliminal cues have unique impact upon our thoughts and emotions. Although we may react to signals noted unconsciously, and Madison Avenue may continue to embed tiny messages in their pictorials, there is no reliable evidence that they attain any special significance. Despite claimed success at movie theaters, flash frames for popcorn do not send us out for some. Properly performed experiments fail to support the peculiar notion that making a sign nearly invisible invests it with unusual power. What we confront in some movies, however, is different and quite inescapable. We may not be entirely conscious of the process, but it requires no subliminal magic tricks. The horrific chiller's remarkable power derives from common imagery and fixed, automatic processes demonstrated beyond doubt. We have been programmed for this presentation.

A systematic survey of the most frightful films reveals their shared ingredients. An archetypal being assaults victims with two-stage destruction: selfhood's dissolution and primal extinction. Always an eroded specter of primitive attack, the agent's appearance furthers both agendas. In all the creature's many guises, indelible features are retained, constant clear messages in three nonverbal languages. On the face alone they spell it all out. Signs of genetic origin announce an animalistic predator unyielding with unnatural needs, set to tear and devour. Learned expressions say that human intelligence directs perverse desires, and we are held in contempt. Symbols of psychic invention tell of a consumptive being with all else erased, now looking to return us to nothing. Told to our surreal subconscious, irrational powers and possibilities are sure to be suggested.

These simple sign languages speak louder than words. Words can add disturbing details, and they may be spoken with unsettling emotion, but the remarkable reach of a horror film's message is lost in translation. Communications should be seen, and primal signals are most striking. Before reaching conscious consideration, they have already fully informed our primitive perceptions, and more than any mere warning, we are sent those certain sensations of immediate assault.

III. Surrealization

When taken into horrific pictures, we will become part of a place where unnatural thoughts and perceptions are realized. Without any hard evidence of something amiss, eerie uneasiness is all around. When danger finally shows itself, even if completely natural, it will always come with much more. Everything is seen within a simplified universe of pure abstractions, empowered essentials, and supernatural suggestions. We are unwelcomed to a world where surreal realization is assured.

Motion pictures may strive for nightmare, but they must be something else to be reasoned narratives made up of the same meanings to all of us. The screen can replicate dreamlike imagery and action, but it cannot produce our sleeping brain's viewpoint, one that is open to anything, including seamless shifts in settings, situations, and people. Moreover, we would not be enjoying this terrible experience without being awake to the fact that it's only a movie. We are not in a dream state, hypnotized, or regressed. Some other way, often without consent, we have been abducted and carried off to some spot where we and the world are no longer the same. By retracing our impressions we will find the route that we took and where we were taken on these forced flights of fancy in film.

In Black-and-White

Imagine a familiar setting for fear as pictured in an old black-and-white movie. In the cold cast of moonlight, a long-abandoned Victorian home, its weathered bare clapboard now driftwood gray, stands surrounded by black sky. Naked, wind-bent branches sweep stark shadows, long and jagged, across the front side and sagging porch roof, while ashen leaves take flight through pale, uncut grass. Venturing into this dark and colorless interior, empty rooms thick with cobwebs, we see a lone wooden chair beside an open window sitting in a shaft of moonlight. The motionless rectangular area of illumination on the floor, broken by the chair's stretched, still silhouette, is animated by the dance of spectral shadows from a sheer curtain's frayed remains. Suddenly we see someone within the gloom, a dark form with gray face and sunken sockets. While eyes of ice remain frozen in our direction, the mouth widens with a welcoming smile. Without a wait for our response, it takes a backward step, vanishing into darkness.

Here and from the start the viewer will experience haunting sensations that are heightened by black-and-white imagery. The living displays a deathly pallor, while everything else assumes an unnerving life of malignant warnings. Even before any danger is revealed, we envision the unseen. Impenetrable shadows, alive and empty spaces, become hiding places for what will have us or serve as vacant voids, open invitations into nothingness. Review the scene in color and the same place is not the same. The green grass, brown leaves, and that hint of blue in the night's sky create a more comfortable picture by conforming to real-life naturalism. Inside, even the faded pastels of peeling wallpaper, brown floorboards, and the chair's worn remains of forest-green paint bring some relief from a world that was no more than cold light and shadow. We still will be startled by an unsettling appearance, but the sight will not be as terrible.

Disturbing changes can be added by us to some color shockers viewed on television. When you appreciate a good attempt that somehow falls short, seems to have all the elements, but still hasn't grabbed you, kill the color, crank up the contrast, and refocus attention on the screen. As past assessments are set aside, the new look is likely to take hold. The setting is more sinister, the menace more fearsome, and, by some peculiar reversal, the unnatural absence of color makes the overall picture more disconcertingly real. See this effect on a large theatrical screen, one receiving the richness and sharp-edged starkness of black-and-white film, and its striking power is undeniable.

Black-and-white photography has the insidious ability to fill out the frame with anxiety, but it is not inherently disturbing. Quite the contrary. It produces pictures of extraordinary beauty, even dramatically heightens their intensity, and this occurs despite color making most of the world prettier and some of it gorgeous. Among all of the stunning examples in black-and-white photographs, from stark and powerful landscapes to soft and sensual studies of the human form, one would be hardpressed to find a picture that would not be diminished by color. Color is an attractive adornment, but its unnecessary addition detracts the eye from more elemental aspects of beauty.

Distraction is automatic, unavoidable, and experienced even by people who usually prefer color pictures. A glamorous studio portrait with no stronger colors than pink flesh tones and brown hair may soften the strength of what we all find to be most seductive, such as striking features, sensual textures, and pleasing proportions and symmetry. It is not what black-and-white adds, but what the absence of color helps to make clear. Centered attention amplifies attraction, and it is precisely the same for repulsion.

When color is missing we automatically focus on fundamentals, and for frightening pictures these elements are highly evocative. Composition assumes ominous significance in the chiller's confrontational setting. Threatening and threatened forms are juxtaposed, and their height in the frame, their spatial relationship, as well as relative size and attitude, become strongly suggestive of their inter-connectedness and disparate power. Moreover, simple shapes and a few subversive signals provide the whole primal picture, convey the inborn nature and present disposition of both sides, and fully inform us with emotion. Light without color spotlights psychic forms and features, adding to their unnatural strength by best illuminating their disturbing design. We lose all sight of any extraneous, more everyday details. Shapes reduced to their insidious essence are raised to the heights of their archetypal dimensions—embodiments bigger than life, pure and graphic icons powerfully emblematic of their essentials.

With black-and-white photography the undistracted eye finds more force from core elements. Our psyche seeks out symbolic meanings from primal imagery, and such an unusual concentration invests the whole scene with unnatural power. How and what we see are transformed, and we are beginning to see in surrealism. Within a universe unadorned by inessentials, its simple picture is described by a few striking elements, images that speak to primitive and prewired perspectives. Even when we experience this with color, except for some possible splashes of blood, it usually looks pretty much the same. In this stripped-down primal world, color is rarely part of the picture, and even evil and innocence are all black-and-white with no shades of gray.

Looking at black-and-white helps to highlight an altered reality that we see in any good fright film. For the viewer it is both a perceptual process and one of emotion, and neither one is ever free of the other.

Shapes of Sensory Experience

There was a time when every perceived identity took the form of pure sensation. Our entire world, even our own sense of existence, was defined by immediate experience. It was a time when selfhood, so violated by the chiller, was first finding its formation.

We are born wide open to an onslaught of alien stimuli, without the capacity for logic struggling to make order out of chaos. We must even learn to perceive, to see separate shapes within the mix of amorphous impressions. Many of these forms become familiar, and they will connect themselves to every associated experience. For Pavlov's dog, conditioned to link feeding to the sound of a bell, the bell became food, and a biscuit had a distinct ring to it. The salivation response continued not only long after rewards were eliminated, but in the complete absence of any appetite. For us early on, things are very much the same, and everything is inseparable from all of its sensations. The sight of the bottle is combined with parental contact, sensual feelings to lips, pleasant taste, comfort to stomach, the temperature, weight, feel, and smell of the container, and all other impressions. It will be a long time before we form balanced pictures, ones made up of distinctly different properties with their own independent meanings and consequences. Now every identity is simply its whole experience.

Our first definition of selfhood emerges by a similar process. The newborn has no understanding of its own boundaries, responding to internal and external stimuli without regard for their direction. So open to and dependent upon the immediate environment, the infant is less separated than he will ever be again. This, along with the limitations of primitive thinking, makes it more difficult to discover where we stop and everything else begins. And even after we distinguish ourselves, seeing ourselves by what we get, and the world by what it gives, our first and lasting pictures of both sides are mutual reflections.

Boundaries of Existence

Separating our self from a surrounding realm of sensations, we begin to find our own shape, but it comes with a conundrum. We are wholly dependent upon the outside, yet only by boundaries do we gain protection and control. The organic conflict between autonomy and dependence is basic to the human condition. Reflected in the needs of society and each of us, it will be acutely felt in adolescence, the next period in our lives where defining personal identity is a principal focus. Here in infancy, however, selfhood is experienced on a purely sensory level, and personal space is a matter of survival. Without boundaries we are lost in a state of sensory confusion, and contradictory impressions of isolation and assault join forces. This may be the permanent condition of an infant who, by inborn dysfunction or social deprivation, is unable to perceive a safe and separate world. It is the total detachment and terror of anyone who, by suffering a breakdown of personal boundaries, encounters extreme psychosis. Being isolated and being overtaken are peculiarly the same, and they may come together by stimulus deprivation.

Floating in a dark and silent chamber of body-temperature water provides a complete separation from the outside that many find wonderfully relaxing, but terror may eventually fill the void. Stimulus isolation can produce increasingly disturbing disorientation and overpowering hallucinations. There is a primal destruction of self by a sensory assault from inside. Even on a level of pure sensation, being a part of, as well as apart from, our environment is essential. Moreover, the experience of absolute isolation is remarkably like its opposite, total exposure. In both instances, we are consumed. In our everyday world, when lacking separation, we become overwhelmed by uncontrollable and meaningless impressions from beyond. When denied these external stimuli in the chamber, we encounter a similar siege from inside. The equivalence of opposites is not without reason. There are no boundaries, no sense of self, no inside or out, only sensory experience of a like nature. The line between isolation and invasion requires a critical act of balance, precarious as walking the high wire, where, if one leans too far to either side, the outcome is pretty much the same.

The horrific chiller has but one theme, the destruction of personal boundaries. First by dissolution, then by primal extinction, what was ourselves vanishes into an alien void. Losing connectedness, control, and understanding, victims experience the opposing sides of our primal conflict. Scenes of separation and assault leave us lost and found within the nothingness of consumption.

Reduction to Rudimentary Understandings

A developed brain cannot be returned to an earlier condition, but film may evoke different states of mind. We won't lose all reason, but our capacity for irrational thought can be stimulated. More sophisticated understandings are still with us, but they are employed to produce simple renderings of primitive conflict. Visual signals trigger commanded response, and their languages speak to the irrational, symbolic sectors of our mind, now set to see psychic significance.

By engaging our unconscious, we best enjoy the richness of the whole design. Primal conflict plays out within a surreal landscape. Anything viewed inside this setting is sculptured by symbolic meanings and primitive emotion. Surreal conceptions become physical realities, and even naturalistic events come with uncanny suggestions. Depending upon context and imagery, a more ordinary danger or injury might convey a sense of being reduced, nullified, drained, taken apart, absorbed, consumed, or wholly altered. Still able to remind ourselves that we are safely seated in front of a screen, we have also arrived at that innermost place where dreamscapes and nightmares are found.

Primal Vision

While extending our own boundaries to the screen, we watch them systematically destroyed in others. Entity and events assault selfhood and, simply on sight, danger may reach inside us with sensations of things to come. It is a most primitive perspective, similar to a time when our own self was first establishing rudimentary roots. Shapes of sensory experience were in primal opposition and our separation from the outside was still uncertain in this realm of unfathomable powers. We arrive at a similar spot in the chiller, a world where our existence is seemingly the sole focus, and we lie exposed and helpless. Forms take the shape of sensation with compelled response, and all of the oppositions will come together and apart in primitive disarray. It goes farther than the oft-noted likeness to childhood fears. Logic, circumstances, and states of being create a scenario along the lines of our earliest understandings.

Examining what we see in black-and-white finds us centered on a dynamic design. It can come in color, highlighted by lighting and composition, a few bold strokes that will capture our attention. If not boldly out front, the imagery is cloaked within more comfortable camouflage, and it will always be the same thing—opposing forms simply described by a small number of signs, signals of automatic emotion. A sparse design provides a whole rendering of confrontation, its character and present standing. Centered attention and psychic significance reinforce one another, resetting our eyes for further signs and symbols. Focus, urgency, and a sense of surrealism take hold. Seen with altered eyesight and understandings, such a distilled composition of invasive designs has changed the very nature of perception.

Advancing our earliest conflict and perspectives with some higher learning, we experience a simulation of nightmares that are not overly dreamlike. Primal vision discovers a monolithic and malignant universe, one unnaturally narrowed to its dark and undeniable dimensions. Powerless to alter the world we have entered, a place solely composed of personal warnings and involuntary directives, even our own self signals its slow dissolution into emptiness.

IV. Entrapment

Horrific chillers leave no witnesses unharmed. Spectators of primal conflict somehow assume its condition. The genre, of course, is by no means unique in fostering a sense of personal participation and evoking related emotions. Given the desperate circumstances encountered here, it is no surprise that they are felt with unusual force. This still does not account for why a predicament may be understood at a safe distance or take us entirely. It turns out that just a few elements set the stage for us, and once these are seen, even situations beyond belief may bear the stamp of real experience. They will also create illusions that last well outside the theater. Even after sober reflection, when we attempt to determine our place in the picture, false impressions continue to play tricks on us.

Illusions of Involvement

More than any other successful director of melodrama, Alfred Hitchcock consciously centered his craft on entrapment. His stories set on innocents ensnared by circumstances, and his plot was to capture the complicity of his unwitting audience. The technique is tension, not necessarily fright, but any type of alarm within unresolved situations. It might be no more than watching an unfamiliar character rushing to make a train for unknown reasons, yet somehow suffering every delay of traffic with him. It could also be a sense of insidious anxiety from adventurous intrigue that would normally be enjoyed at a safe distance. Less often, but with no doubt, it was horror. Hitchcock expressed little interest in intellectual mystery, knowing that such matters do little to make it our story. He even found the final outcome, assumed so important to us, to be far less significant than the circumstances themselves. Suspense is our connection, tension from watching people in situations that have unwanted possibilities. It was always this way, his trademark and means of engagement, and it proves to be the prime formula for involvement all sorts of situations. Introduce danger, and it becomes our own. The process surely works, but our accepted understandings are not so certain.

Hitchcock provides the example of seeing two men innocently engaged in idle conversation not knowing that a time bomb has been set to detonate in fifteen minutes. He observed that they remain fearless while we suffer the situation with high anxiety, and that our experience will be more profound than the shock of a completely unexpected explosion. Though true, this seems to defy explanation. Our anxiety appears to exceed its source. Disaster is some time away and it may not even occur, but our disturbance is greater than the worst possible outcome. We need not be given anything else or sense more than we get, but a distant bark is unaccountably worse than the bite.

Our understanding reveals another confusion. When watching people headed for possible loss, we are likely to credit ourselves with concern for their well-being. Seeing that our suffering is extended to little-liked characters, we may deem it to be some innate form of empathy. Neither account, however, explains what aspect of the person's condition provokes our distress. It is not a sympathetic response to their feelings. The sight of someone frightened is harmless unless we see the source. Even if it is a favorite character possessed by terror, we are not moved to his state without sharing the trigger. Our friend suffers without us while the happy couple beside the bomb creates disturbance. All this suggests the possibility that our concern is for what may happen. We are reminded, however, that the facts prove otherwise. The men's demise may mean little to us, and witnessing an explosion is less disturbing than watching the wait.

Although we may have no attachment to characters on-screen, there is no denying their central role. The bomb is harmless on its own, and it is the same for any threat that is not visually dreadful. All experience is by way of a target. We may see a close-up of the weapon, but sensations of assault await the walk-on of a potential victim. If this is empathy, it exhibits peculiarities. Our distress is not tied to the person's present feelings or future well-being. Where we become completely connected is not entirely clear.

Our confusions stem from a failure to separate two independent presentations. In every form of theatrical pictures we come to care for individuals and share their concern with unfolding events. In some genres, most notably the fright film, we also participate to the point of experiencing the action within ourselves. This process is deeper and more direct, unshakable and unavoidable. These two levels of involvement often appear together and are likely to be seen as one, but they are separate impressions arising from two distinct presentations. Everything defining horrific chillers takes hold at the deeper level of physical and psychic experience. For primal conflict or any disturbance to hurt us, certain conditions have been staged. When we fix our attention on the present standing of a menaced target, all apparent contradictions vanish.

The Web of Present Perceptions

While watching the men chat near to the bomb, we certainly wish that they would move and may even feel the foolish impulse to warn them. Our desire for their departure, however, is strictly self-centered and restricted to the immediate moment. Our only goal is to escape the personal pain produced by the present imagery. We watch and experience intolerable inaction in the face of closing destruction, and we are slowly consumed by the sensation of complete impotence before easily escaped extinction. So long as the people remain in place and we stay by their side, it is the one sensation we cannot shake loose. What we see is what we get, and it is always so. Our distress will be from assuming the momentary state of a figure in respect to a visible, nearby force, and it is the only conflict found to be contagious. We are collateral victims solely of immediate imagery. We need not look to the future. The assault has already begun.

Comparing our response to the time bomb with a similar sequence reveals how the rules are fixed. Both examples begin with the culprit, his weapon, and detailed plans of destruction. The setup is the same, and only the contents of the canister are different. The first holds conventional explosives. The second is set to release an odorless, ghastly vapor. We learn that it produces the violent constriction characteristic of strychnine, but the victim will live for some minutes. Worse still, as the face becomes swollen and twisted with pain, layers of tissue will begin to burst, peel, and fall away. It surely is a horrific prospect, but so far safely beyond the picture. Until we see differently, both sequences will provide identical experience.

Neither scene is painful to watch while an endangered person is missing. Even the second version provides no more than plot. The sight of the assassin or his deadly weapon fails to trigger any feeling of personal assault. Detailed wording of the poison's terrible consequences sound to be horrifying, but they are short on a sense of participation. Even planting the canister in some public place merely sets the stage. We may know the identity of the target, but our entrapment awaits seeing him in place. We will be safe so long as there is only the danger.

Villains and victims work only in tandem. As soon as the couple settles beside the explosives, we assume enormous anxiety for uncared-for characters, and the formerly unfelt menace is viewed with unavoidable alarm. The personal experience continues to be the same from viewing both sequences. We watch the second more mindful of what we may be forced to witness, but these concerns are not part of our present condition. It is the sight of idleness next to destruction that destroys our composure, and it feels no different even in the face of far more fearsome execution. Even cutting away to the new canister is the same. Just as the unexploded bomb triggers no feeling of being blown apart, seeing the other weapon forwards no sensation of our threatened future. Both shots simply and concisely magnify the tension created by the couple's position, jolting us with a heightened sense of urgency. For now the two scenes present identical behavior in the same situation with visually alike weapons. Any differences that count are safely free from sight.

When what was withheld becomes part of present perceptions, the two presentations part company. Once again we suffer only what we see and hear, and explosives do their most damage before detonation. When they go off, we are hit by the shock of sudden agitation, but the commotion soon settles into a sense of overall relief. We certainly are sorry that innocent people have been killed, but, from the standpoint of our insides, it is far better than seeing them alive in such jeopardy. This weapon's second stage was too swift and invisible for us to share much of the assault. Beyond the unusually short time span, the blast provides virtually no visual impression of a person in the process of destruction. We are not so lucky, however, with the second canister. The rapid erosion of the person's face, soon revealing portions of the skull, is a horrific portrait of selfhood's passage, protracted and personally painful. Explosion may have done the same to the other victim, but not for our eyes. With the gas we see dissolution and primal extinction drawn with the reflexive imagery of involuntary emotion, and what was no more than a gruesome prospect free of its experience becomes a dreadful assault on our insides.

Scenes of suspense typically foreshadow a far greater disturbance, adding to the illusion that we experience tremors of an anticipated future. When our worries are worse than the dreaded event, it makes clear that our involvement is with the present picture, not a preview of coming attractions. The sight of blindness to mortal danger is far worse than one of a quick and easy final exit. Our response may be completely contrary to our overall attachment to the victims, to their emotions, and to our anxiety over possible outcomes, and it may bear no resemblance to the form of upcoming assault. Suspense while waiting is as immediate as physical attack so long as people and threatening forces are closely connected. It does not matter whether the nearby menace is frozen in stealth or already striking. When watching the two sides in place, we experience direct attack. Our condition automatically assumes a momentary perceived standing. We need not imagine any more than what we see, and it will make no difference if we do. We are solely in the hands of present perceptions.

Of course, not all concerns are so set. We develop a form of attachment to some individuals that extends to action off-screen and beyond the present. We also consider our own future, worrying about what may be in store for us. Such free-floating anxieties, however, command neither the depth nor character of core experience. Concerns about what we may be forced to face heightens the context for terror, but only immediate imagery creates experience. Knowledge of our friend's unseen misfortunes or demise may make us unhappy, but we are spared from taking part. We certainly will be more distressed to watch tragedy befall a liked character than some unknown, but it is the pain of personal assault that overwhelms us, and this remains very much the same. Participation is confined to primal elements, and just a few triggers of personal experience embedded within the scene create the illusion of being there. Placed squarely in the midst of conflict, even when people aren't like us and don't know what we do, we still may feel to be them.

Entrapment at the movies is woven from present perceptions, a web linking someone to forces in proximate space. Strung to ensnare viewer and victim alike, it instantly ties us to the point of entanglement and wires us with trembling sensations of our present position. Lines of action laid beyond the web's fabric do not become entwined in its tensions. Despite what we may imagine, foreseen events yet to be spun cannot touch us. Not even our feelings for the victim make a connection. The only ties that bind are drawn by the trap's tangible construction, and we are shaken by the inescapable agitations of being in that particular spot.

In horror films we are prey in the grip of a terribly disturbing presence, a ghastly, devouring creature at the center of its snare. More entangled, further disarmed and disabled, we will feel the tremors of our annihilator's approach. Suddenly seen, it need come no closer to take hold of our insides. Soon it will be all over us as we find ourselves at the center of engulfment, bound up and undone.

V. Rules of Engagement

Seeing a frightening film a second time around, we are often impressed by its undiminished impact. We might have expected this from powerful scenes of deadly assault, but did not anticipate being so upset by the same false alarms or by stalking that will conclude with no contact. Surprise from being twice victimized credits us with reasoned responses. It also suggests the belief that signs of possible attack are something quite separate from images of unleashed assault. Our psyche makes no such distinctions, and it sees each place of jeopardy apart from our understanding of what happens later. Spotting predator and prey closely linked in the pose of primal aggression triggers a sense of similar standing within us. Physical contact need not be witnessed to perceive the two sides in the locked embrace of confrontation. We feel its sensations without having to think, and knowing some reason to feel otherwise still may not save us. All clear and closely cast positions of primal conflict return us to the innocent moment. There are no false alarms. Our loss is all there and happening now, and its true shape may successfully survive being seen time and time again.

Physical participation in fright films stems from a singular set of circumstances. A scene-by-scene inspection of defining moments uncovers a simple picture of shared dimensions. Situations may have to be assembled with the aid of intellect, but whatever complexities we may see or choose to consider, predicaments will be reduced to a few elements with rules for our reaction. Only two factors secure our engagement, and no more than three others may be added to our fright.

Founding Factors

Proximate stalking or lying in wait, the shrinking distance of attack, and the direct contact of physical assault are merely different positions in a singular continuum of confrontation. They all present what we will always see, a pictured collision of opposing forces.

Someone is seen to be countered, and their state of *reduced standing* is the first factor in our condition. The power of the threat is measured against the endangered person's reaction, and this is multiplied by the importance of what is being threatened. The disturbance may be mortal danger, lesser physical peril, or merely an impediment to personal goals. Its power may be partially blocked or completely unanswered. Limited to present perceptions, all that counts is the resultant net standing. We view moment-by-moment portraits of unmatched strength, disruptions that can differ widely in force and independent importance, and the stress we feel is from assuming that position.

The second required factor is *perceived proximity* of the disturbance. Emotion felt from taking a given position is multiplied by how closely both sides of the conflict are seen to be connected. Viewing the scene of a hidden time bomb, we feel a bit better when somebody stands up and shows signs of leaving. Instead of increasing his distance, however, he shortens it, sitting back down on a sealed chest containing the explosives. Now our eyes are riveted on the spot, and the sight delivers a rush of added anxiety. A blast will take everyone out, and ground zero should be the least painful position, but due to its disturbing closeness to the weapon, this is without question the most frightening place to see occupied. *Physical proximity* is always counted. When the time of closing contact is known in advance or is suggested by the enemy's behavior, the dreadful ticking of *temporal proximity* is added to the multiplier.

Our automatic and deepest anxiety from situations on-screen springs from two essential factors. A victim must be seen to be connected to a visualized threat, and the negative force must be close. We will experience the stress of having this reduced standing, and whenever proximity is increased or decreased, the level of discomfort is sure to follow.

Optional Additions

Some threats, by elements of their imagery, assault us with unnerving sensations. These disturbing designs may be independent of any physical ability to do us harm, and they send very different impressions. The opposition becomes an additional factor by presenting primal signatures. *Opposing signatures of dissolution* are displayed by an unnatural void of facial features, limited range of expressions, and mechanical movements that may include a slowed step. Coupled with signs of hostility, they are seen as an awful inhumanity, empowering the embodiment by the absence of any other feelings or focus, and we will also sense this dissolution within ourselves. *Opposing signatures of aggression* signal oppression or primal extinction. Raised up and inflated, poised and ready, is an oppressive sign of dominance that triggers submission and sensations of lost power. The most primal sign of extinction, sharp shredders surrounding an open cavity, send shivers of quick dissolution and total consumption. Signatures of these two stages may also be sent by sound. If sudden, deep thrusts from a switchblade come with calm utterances spoken in a matter-of-fact manner, the agent's dissolution of humanity is terribly discomposing. Should the same insertions arrive with animalistic shrieks, our sense of primitive extinction is amplified.

All of this imagery comes together in the most terrifying realization of nightmares, the archetypal horrific being. Frightening forms are usually living or resurrected, but they can be no more than something material. A menace may embody all of the signatures, show some, or have none. Villains often provide part of the picture by a dissolute face along with oppressive size and posture, but lack features of bestial annihilation. A human with hideous plans but no psychic signs, however, adds nothing to the sensed threat. Mechanical objects have similar range. They may appear benign to our eyes, such as the canister of horrific gas, or bring a full complement of fearsome symbols. An unmanned, inner-directed bulldozer seen relentlessly grinding toward us whatever way we run, repeatedly raising bladed jaws high overhead before slamming them to the ground with resounding force, surely presents a broad spectacle of primal alarms.

Another optional pair of primal signatures may be placed on the other side of the conflict, and they, as well, will compound anxiety with dreadful sensations. *Assumed signatures of dissolution* may mark the victim with signs of diminished capacity or voided personal appearance. Incompleteness begins with the reduction of normal abilities: the loss of power, awareness, and understandings. It may come to a display of incomplete appearance when, by injury or transformation, there is a voiding of features most felt to be self. *Assumed signatures of primal extinction* show our complete disappearance in a primitive fashion. It may be a form of elemental erasure or, more often, a bestial assault obliterating personal features and extinguishing capacity. Sometimes there need be no more than the elimination of one capacity, the ability to be or remember who we are. Within the world of science fiction or the supernatural, total loss may be the erasure of our insides while preserving a functioning shell.

Primal signatures on either side of confrontation may be merely symbolic, and even if altering the balance of power, they will be felt beyond their actual effect. Reduced personal power feels worse than the loss of a weapon. It is also worse than an equivalent gain in the opposition. Anxiety is raised, and its character is more unsettling. Reduction of self is so central that extreme peril may never become overpowering without it.

Primal signatures may also be found in the setting: disturbing sights and sounds that create *surrounding impressions of conflict.* Although having more punch when part of the confrontation, signatures on the outside do make an impression. The atmosphere that we feel simply by seeing and hearing the setting will become infused in what takes place. The spot, redefined by the framing of each new angle on the scene, can heighten anxiety and even bring more troubling perspectives. How the space is set can be a factor. It may be oppressive, with towering forms looming over us and reaching out with foreboding shapes and shadows. It can isolate us either by constrictive enclosure or with an empty expanse of desolation and decay, and any alteration of space will weaken personal boundaries. One way or another, the symbolic space may stand ready to consume us, and even familiar territory turns into alien ground. The photographic style will play its part by composition, texture, and use or absence of color. Background music may move us with formless agitations or by a more finely tuned resonance that carries the dimensions of disturbance. Forces of nature, bestial, mechanical, or surreal forms can be suggested, and so can the menace's mood. Tempo sets our spot in the continuum of conflict from stealth through the quickening pulse of pursuit (*Jaws*) to the strident discords of attack (*Psycho*).

This fifth factor and the other two options are all that fright films can add to bare conflict. Each factor is measured along limited lines and creates its own sensations without regard to a better understanding of portrayed events. Presentations may be artfully woven, but the audience's undoing is tied to pure formula.

Equation of Altered States

When conflict on-screen becomes reproduced within ourselves, we will have equated our own shape with a conditional calculation. It requires that we are seeing someone diminished by external forces, and it fixes our feelings by set formulations. Our *participatory experience* is always the product of present perceptions and no more than the same five factors. The strength and nature of *reduced standing* creates organic stress, and this alarm is multiplied by *perceived proximity.* Three optional factors introduce psychic anxiety into the equation. Fear is compounded by unnatural dread when either side of conflict has primal signatures. The negative force may carry *opposing signatures of dissolution* and/or *aggression.* The reduced person may be marked with *assumed signatures of dissolution* or *primal extinction.* The setting can present the same imagery or its sound imprint. Although this fifth factor is not a multiplier, *surrounding impressions of conflict* can be added.

P.E. = (R.S.) (P.P.) (1 + O.S.D. + A.) (1 + A.S.D. + P.E.) + (S.I.C.)

This formulation makes no attempt at mathematical precision. It does provide the proven prime elements of core experience, and by computed strength and character well expresses our equation with what we see. Every viewer will employ it, and it is also available to the writer. Used to reenvision an ordinary scene of assault, the transformation can turn it to terror.

Various terms of engagement are easily pictured in a military movie. It is nighttime, and our soldier sits alone in an isolated tent trying to unjam his only weapon. We cut to enemy headquarters where plans to shell the area are being completed. Despite some concern for our man's welfare and detailed descriptions of the whole operation, we have yet to become directly involved. This comes with a message received at a hilltop bunker, orders to fire their cannons at midnight. Now cutting back and forth between tent and bunker, we are decidedly in the mix and placed on the wrong side. Figure and proximate forces are visually connected, and our concern for someone's future becomes personal and present alarm.

Time is beginning to count, but our man is in no hurry while he methodically works on a weapon that cannot possibly save him here. He tries it again, finds it still jammed, and scratches his head. Parting the tent flaps, he steps out into the night, lights a cigarette, and inhales deeply. Looking out across the moonlit landscape his eyes end up on the distant rise of land where the bunker lies hidden. His gaze continues in that direction for a few more puffs, then turns to the tent. Ten minutes to midnight, and back inside it is becoming a bit nerve-racking watching him calmly reexamine the gun. Our discomfort is suddenly disrupted by the jolt of the flaps flying open and seeing an armed enemy there. A quick scuffle and lucky punch by our side, and our man makes a break for the woods. We are running along with him, our adrenaline pumping, while he frantically tries to activate his weapon. Now the enemy is somewhere behind us, also running headlong through thick woods that deny any sense of how close he might be. Suddenly the end is in sight, but not a good one. Woods end at an open expanse with no place to hide. The enemy has arrived and, still attempting to fix his weapon, our soldier doubles over in a blast of gunfire.

Engagement in combat pictures may entail unsettling suspense, shock, and breathless high anxiety. When it's over, however, it's over. Like a good soldier we quickly recover, ready to return to action. This is not what we feel in a horror film, left badly shaken, not really wanting to face the next skirmish. Our short scenario is good for combat experience, but no more. To punch it up with more emotions, we turn to the formula of five factors.

For starters, we can make far better use of the proximity factor. Move the enemy up close, hiding in darkness outside the tent, waiting to toss a grenade at the appointed time. Everything is the same but for a spatial proximity that is irrelevant to the time and manner of attack. If there is any difference in danger, there is now a greater chance that it will be discovered before it's too late, yet seeing the enemy separated by just a few feet and a thin piece of canvas is decidedly more disturbing than the sight of his distant counterpart. Our sensations prove to be less tied to logical connections than perceived linkages. A mile away, man and missile are seen at a safer distance than if they are already waiting in the wings. It also makes it possible to bring the assailant all the way. Trade the grenade for his hands and complete the proximity with a personal contact that is more powerful than shrapnel.

Should we be able to include them, primal signatures may be as important as close proximity. Here there is opportunity for their appearance on both sides. Inside at work on the weapon and outside scanning the scene, we have made a good start with nonawareness, but we can add another signature while maintaining the balance of forces. Instead of the firearm, we find him tending to a painful foot. Not only when needed, but sitting right here, impairment of self is more troubling than a malfunctioning weapon. On the other side we can add signatures of dissolution and primal aggression, dreadful additions to what remains the same situation. We spot a dark figure in the night, keeping close to the ground, slowly worming its way toward the tent. Arriving in stealth, it settles silently a short distance away, and suddenly we see that face we have seen before. Unusually barren with mismatched eyes, and a branching scar cutting completely across it, it has the look of lifeless pieces improperly assembled. To remain undetected, this commando trades explosives for the silent treatment, and the last time we saw him he silenced someone by tearing the man's jaw off and ripping his throat out. Now the mere suggestion of his shadow on the canvas creates a chilling aura of his awful presence. Seen full face in the doorway it will be terrifying.

When it comes to the chase, the formula suggests many changes. Thick woods nicely create anxious uncertainty about our distance, but it is stronger to perceive sure connections, especially when the distance is shrinking. Switch the woods to an open field and swamp where we can see it all happening. Our man is running quickly, but his injury is slowing him down, and the enemy is closing the gap. This sight is worse than seeing him trying to work the weapon. Both heighten concerns that he will be undone, but with personal impairment the process has begun.

Once in the water on equal footing, he is able to slosh or swim as fast as his pursuer. Despite this turn for the better, the scene becomes more disturbing. Soon deep in mud and waist high in water, he finds each step an effort and forward motion slowed. There is something horrific about being so unnaturally sluggish, having all of our efforts make so little difference, being drained of all energy when nothing else matters. The enemy also moves in slow motion at the same pace, but that dehumanized face is so smugly at ease that simply keeping our distance doesn't seem to count for much. Even our man's appearance becomes a bit frightful. Flailing their way through swamp and underbrush, the two muddied bodies have assumed a disconcerting resemblance. The victim's face is erased by muck and slime, his matted hair entangled with weeds, and skin scratched and cut by thorny branches. He is on his way to being one with the specter of negation behind him. Scrambling across a log into a boggy area, he suddenly finds himself stuck and steadily sinking deeper and deeper. Slowly disappearing and unable to move forward, he grasps for the log. He sees the enemy approaching, then the outstretched arm and that hand across his face. We need to see no more for the whole sequence to be far more disturbing than the one that ended with his death, and it would remain that way even if he makes a clean, if muddied, getaway.

Core experience springs from inborn measurements of threat. The trick for terror is to heighten the calculation's unreasoned component, and to engage our unconscious with signals of related anxieties. Our fight-or-flight response evolved for nature's nearby dangers, and proximity can fool us by entering the equation as an irrational factor. Unrealistic levels of anxiety will arise from maximizing proximity, such as putting the enemy so near to the tent. If our assailant must use a gun, it's a bad idea merely to aim it at a distance. Jam it under the cringing guy's chin, or even better, thrust it a few inches into his mouth.

Once we start adding optional factors, threat will be felt far beyond reason, and the added sensation will be more dreadful. Either side of the conflict will be factored again when they display primal signatures. Here the enemy can come with a facial makeover as well as some unpleasant memories. His mismatched pieces of an empty face aimed at us, decomposition recomposed our direction, are chilling additions without posing an additional threat. Introducing a prior first impression of him, that time he tore someone's face apart, horrifically centers his assault upon selfhood. Signatures on the other side unsettle us further. The loss of a fully functioning leg is figured into *reduced standing*, as was the jammed weapon, but it is counted again in the fourth factor as a sensation of selfhood's reduction. When flight turns into slow motion, our face becomes one with the other, and we soon find ourselves sinking, by way of pictured decomposition, vanishing power and appearance, we experience the primal dissolution of ourselves.

Assumed Position

A powerful sense of personal experience distinguishes fright films. We may become highly involved in other narratives, concerned and closely connected, but we remain observers. A wide range of emotions may be experienced, but still it is not our story. We are more likely to be lost in the illusion of participation when watching films of forced tension. Here the sensation is so deep and undeniably real, so immediate and full of personal warning, that we may have to remind ourselves of our safe separation, and given where horror films take their aim on us, it's hard to imagine a more self-centered experience.

The crafting of a strong sense of place, all of the sights and sounds of some real location, helps to put us on the spot, and this complete impression of being there is usually credited for our feeling of personal danger. The reverse, however, is also true and even more powerful. A small number of signals trigger emotion, feelings so certain that we must be there, and this impression is validated by the whole fleshed-out picture.

When following threatened characters, we usually feel that we stand in their place, but our position is rarely the same, and the stress can be quite different. Seeing someone stabbed makes us wince with each blow, yet our sensation stops just short of the cut. We suffer the victim's increasingly diminished position, while safe from other visceral repercussions. Being a third party limits what we share, but it also adds its own troubling perspectives. In the most effective scenes time is best spent near to the losing side, sometimes through their eyes, but never restricting ourselves to their point of view. Some films have attempted to enhance our presence by employing the camera to represent the central character, but it turns out to have the opposite effect. This positioning is misdirected, even when well handled. To assume a position, we best see it taken, seeing the whole person with their posture and attitude facing opposition. Sometimes a separate place is the only possible spot, such as the one where we suffer somebody's blindness to what we see coming. We may stand with the victim but never walk in their shoes. Whenever we find ourselves on-screen, limited perspectives are connecting us. We assume a state seen solely by instinctive perceptions and our symbolic psyche.

We will always side with the losing side unless the loss is well deserved. Having taken that position, we will see things differently. Depending upon who has them, the same signatures may be given opposite meanings, the sure signs of a winner or a loser. Absence of expressive features on the threatening side is seen as unnatural emptiness and inhumanity, and it strengthens any dreadful desires by erasing everything else. Even reduction of physical or mental ability, seen in the extreme with the living dead, only adds to the impression that it can't be stopped. The victim, however, enjoys no gain in this loss. Missing features or abilities are evidence of our expiration. If there are surreal forces, their use is sure to be one-sided. Location is everything in this world of exact opposites. Our side and the outside are composed of two states in opposite conditions. Coming together in confrontation, they combine as complementary forms of the same design.

Although it comes without thinking, our reduced position is carefully calculated. A fixed formulation figures the power and nature of loss, and it makes for our inclusion so long as we see both sides. We may have some involvement with someone's story and worry about what may happen, but participation awaits the sight of some negative force. Conversely, villains without victims are powerless. Ordinary-looking danger does not touch us, and even frightening forms miss their mark. Remove a monster from confrontation, watch it going about unrelated activities, and even the fearsome sight of that awful face begins to pale. If either founding factor is missing, turns out to be zero, their multiple comes to nothing. Even the added fifth factor will not amount to much. Suspenseful atmosphere and music will work for a while, but with no confrontation to cling to, these surrounding impressions soon add up to no more than an irritating dissonance with what we are watching.

When we see conflict on-screen and find ourselves there, participation follows a fixed formula. In our conditional calculation, all circumstances are reduced to naked confrontations. The two founding factors of experience employ only a few elements from the picture, create simple conflict, and set a level of undifferentiated anxiety. Two optional multipliers, if present, compound organic alarm with chilling concerns for selfhood. Frightening rushes of nature's adrenaline are tainted by impurities of unnatural dread. Finally, surrounding impressions of conflict may be added, coloring profound experience, but not making it.

Conflict is the center of most narrative pictures, including comedy. All high-tension genres must conform oppositions to the rules of engagement, featuring a powerful and important, nearby disturbance. How they fill out the rest of the equation fixes their impact and may determine their category. Disaster films typically take their toll of the cast with little harm to the audience. Their natural or man-made disasters usually lack a center with primal signatures, and victims most often depart without the slow erasure of self or a disintegrating disappearance. Action-adventure films may provide more thrills, but they tend to be free of chilling sensation. The menace is evil, but not particularly primal, and more often than not protagonists rise above our normal abilities rather than being reduced. Progressing to films of shock, dread, and horror, the forces will display bold psychic signatures of negation and obsessive aggression, and a reduced person will be marked by selfhood's dissolution and its primitive consumption. These films will also add similar signatures to the surrounding environment. And all of this combines into the genre's complete experience. Coming fully loaded with all the options, the equation of altered states provides the whole formula.

VI. In a Moment

Inside a frozen moment, still matters may not be static. The motionless picture may be transformed by what we saw earlier, and it can change right before our eyes by what we find from continued viewing.

Reinforcing Connections

Our experience from watching idle talk near to a time-bomb grows by strengthening connections, and it becomes increasingly intense without introducing any new elements. The sequence may be no more than an assembly of the same three shots, cutting back and forth between couple, canister, and clock, but its impact becomes highly magnified. Well before the appointed time the clock does not change in any significant respect, and it will never present any surprises. Until the end the weapon will remain frozen in place and in appearance, and the people continue to show no signs of moving. Although these constant images stay very much the same, they change while we are watching. Long before the time begins to count, cutaways to the creeping clock and static weapon become increasingly disturbing.

This expanding emotion is not simply the result of being worked up in a temporary state of cumulative alarm. The picture may cut to another location, allowing us to become considerably calmed, but it will make no difference upon our return. The sight of people still there instantly activates the advanced anxiety of our departure. Our disturbance is not where we were a moment ago, or where it all began. It remains determined by the degree by which the imagery of conflict has reinforced its own bonds.

This process is a matter of making perceptual connections linking visual elements of the scene, and its power is retained for some time. Although the weapon is not frightening to look at, and where it is placed makes no difference, it is far more effective to see the canister than only know of its presence. Only by union with one another do the individual images of the couple and clock, and even the menacing bomb, assume sensation, and cross-cutting serves to strengthen connecting fears. Eventually, closing minutes will create a true emergency, and its heightening proximity will be dramatically felt. From the start, however, without seeing anything new, our sense of urgency is quickly expanding. With the cementing of connections, our anxiety may be more related to how long we have been watching than to how little time is left.

Encompassing Possibilities

Static situations can change in more than intensity. They may even shift in nature by making us reappraise everything that we see. Something symbolic of threat finds support in other parts of the scene, and suddenly the same picture presents a brand-new array of forces and feelings.

Without any hint of a frightful future, a film opens with a wide shot within the quiet confines of a church at night, dimly lit with some illumination from clusters of candles placed off to the sides. A solitary woman, head bowed, sits silently in a pew. A man enters from outside, lights a candle, then genuflects and crosses himself when facing the altar.

Cutting closer, we see that the man is lost in thought, possibly a bit troubled, and he gives no indication of even noticing the person in the pew behind him as he takes a seat. A short time passes, and the previously motionless woman slowly lifts her head. There is almost no face. The smooth skin is onion-white and translucent. There is no mouth, only embryonic indications of a nose, and the eyes are mere slits of pulled-back skin. Seeing this specter of voided self fix on the unseeing figure so closely at hand is instantly chilling, and we are experiencing an immediate sense of primal endangerment.

Significantly, our alarm occurs with no signs of assault. Seen in isolation, the face need not be menacing. It is highly disturbing, possibly grotesque, but it displays unnatural emptiness without aggression. Lacking this face, however, the identical situation evokes no anxiety. An expressionless look from an ordinary woman would not suggest the slightest enmity, and it might even appear to be quietly compassionate. Despite such assurances, the more that we watch this formless face fix on the figure within reach, the more certain we become of its malice. We perceive a most sinister force targeted upon an unaware innocent, and our agitation grows from his failure to see it. Should viewers not have known what form of film to expect, they now brace themselves for horror.

The frozen encounter continues to expand, incorporating other elements of the picture, including formerly pleasant pieces of imagery. The church's confinement and flickering candlelight become a confirmation of our fears, no more comforting parts of a supportive setting. Moreover, the longer the two people remain still, the greater the likelihood that the shape of their engagement is transformed. The absent face that assumed malevolence may now appear to reach beyond itself, encompassing the man in its aura. He has fallen victim to some form of surreal assault. His intolerable stillness, his continued failure to turn and see this awesome absence of humanity, begins to support the impression of his own powerlessness and consumption, and we see his self and personal boundaries being sucked away by the emptiness behind him.

Without any evidence of threat, in a quiet setting with peaceful expectations, we experience endangerment. The woman makes no expression of animosity, but her face's unnatural incompleteness, so barren of all expression, evokes frightful possibilities, and such proximity to somebody's blind side instinctively calls for alarm. The visual arrangement is too set for assault and the face too symbolically powerful in its negation for this picture of possible peril to be overlooked. Gut anxiety seeks out all sources of danger, and what was safe sanctuary becomes oppressive, isolated, dark confinement. The setting sends impressions of separation and loss, and, even though the woman did not select her position, her placement and unseen gaze are now seen to show stealth. Made menacing in a surreal assessment, reviewed within these mutually reinforcing and expanding connections, her psychic signatures of dissolution become the physical threat. Symbolic imagery attached to the woman is impressed upon the man, and we experience his personal diminishment. The now-perceived picture of her nihilistic motives magically becomes both the means and the shape of destruction.

It might be argued that we jump to conclusions from recalling similar situations in other pictures. We have certainly seen it all before. In fact, we never witness entirely different conjoinments in any effective horrific chiller. Psychic shapes occupy the instinctive position of assault, and their terrifying impressions of loss become part of the physical danger. Familiarity with films may stimulate our search for menacing signals or strengthen connections in the making, but it is not the origin of our response. Similar arrangements are always seen because they are the designs of automatic emotion.

When oppositions are forcefully framed together, continued viewing of the same scene will mount in power. If the picture also includes features awaiting a fearful perspective, the swelling sensation may even expand in its nature. Both forms of developing moments are created by time spent watching. Other moments may be instantly enlarged by a time already past.

Linking Associations

Although viewers stay secure from a yet-to-be-seen future, they remain subject to what they witnessed earlier. The present can be changed by carrying impressions from the past. When danger reappears, its strength and even character may differ from first-sighting. A repeat encounter with hidden explosives differs slightly. If they had made a deafening blast, there will be a bit more anxiety. Should they have failed to take victims, more certainty will be necessary this time. The canister holding gas follows the same principles, but it also holds the power to transform how we see it. Once the contents have been released and horrific erosion and consumption are seen, the canister's image is completely altered. As soon as a new victim settles in place, the weapon forwards feelings of its second stage.

The viewer's condition is confined to present perceptions, but the present may contain what came before. Pictures formerly linked to primal experiences will assume sensations of what was seen. They can be added to the static canister or an ordinary-appearing person who was seen stabbing someone in a fit of frenzy. It might simply be the sight of a window if once before it was followed by the sudden snap of a shade and someone crashing through the glass. Subsequent sightings of images closely associated with painful occurrences may bare impressions of what we came to feel. Once the monster in the attic has struck, the aura of its presence encompasses every empty room and hallway. Later, merely a suggestion of it lurking in the shadows evokes sensations of its terrifying visage, the manner of its stalking and striking, and what we lost along the way.

Before any action unfolds, the reappearance of anything connected to an earlier fright will be cause for alarm, and sensations of previous outcomes transform the present picture. Continued viewing of any confrontation will always cement critical connections, causing the scene to grow in strength. Heightening disturbance may even shift its own character by encompassing possibilities within the scene. A menacing viewpoint alters perceptions in a series of self-confirming, symbolic discoveries, and primal signatures in the danger as well as surroundings may turn into forces that begin to re-form people with their own design. From three directions, without a thought, hard evidence or logic, even within a frozen moment, any situation may be subject to change.

VII. Scenes of Disturbance

Moving pictures are a rapid succession of moments that keep circumstances in motion, and they hold our interest by following the course of central characters or main events. Developing situations are essential to frightening films, providing a depth and richness to disturbance by continually changing our condition. Sequences are much more complex than a one-victim snapshot, but they are still confined to the same factors. The web of present perceptions expands in its construction, and more than one form of equated state may be felt at once. From moment to moment, and sometimes in different ways at the same time, we are further reduced and divided into a finished portrait of diminishment.

Changing Conditions

Films featuring tension spend little time standing still, and constant changes take their toll on us. Deepening discomfort is felt from a string of related conflicts, and even from only one line of tension shifting up and down.

A mental patient's assault on a nurse has not been halted by a blinding splash of acid. The woman's flight is stopped, however, by a locked door, and she looks back in terror when the badly burned inmate appears at the far end of the long corridor. Our fear mounts as he feels his way along the wall, slowly moving in the nurse's direction until he reaches the corner of a connecting hallway. He pauses, cocking his head to listen for signs of the silent woman, and then turns down the wrong corridor. For no apparent reason, however, he stops again and returns to his original path toward his frozen victim. The situation is now identical to one that ran a steady course, but the momentary alteration has heightened tension. Changes, unless mostly for the better, increase alarm.

A night watchman could produce the same result. Appearing unexpectedly from an adjoining ward, he heads straight for the locked door. Instead of opening it, however, he merely checks that it is secure and continues on his rounds. The shifting path of a possible savior can substitute for the erratic approach of an assailant. Both directly alter the balance of forces, easing our reduction for a moment before its full return. Varying the strength of disturbance is inherently unsettling. Studies of stress often conclude that uncertainty is a core factor in anxiety. At the movies, if not other places, the term is potentially misleading. Prediction must be part of the picture, and complete ambiguity is meaningless. If enemies are seen moving about similar corridors with no spatial reference to each other, they begin to create more tedium than anxiety. Positions must be clear to be counted. Changing their arrangement is even more damaging. We do not suffer blind uncertainty, rather shifting assessments of the loser's standing.

More upsetting than uneven agitations from one line of tension is the introduction of related anxieties. Should the nurse be fumbling through some keys, trying to find the right one, only to see them drop and scatter across the floor, it adds a frightful breakdown of normal functions to our condition. This particular patient will also make matters feel worse. His blind pursuit with burned-away features forwards impressions of his unnatural obsession as well as those of our own erasure. If he has been seen earlier horrifically assaulting some other victim, he will also carry this imagery with him. All these feelings occur in a place of isolation and exposure with disturbing people and associations, and their surrounding sensations will color the character of every experience.

Confrontations can also change the course of other circumstances. New conflicts intertwine with old ones, becoming part of other pressing predicaments by possibly altering their outcome. The nurse does a good job creating alarm from her increasingly reduced standing, but she also could be employed at the same time in another position. The film's plot might center on a series of mysterious deaths that turn out to involve some doctors. The nurse has phoned the main character, telling him she has the answer, and he is on his way. Now her possible demise rekindles an additional conflict, one that has been our principal cause for alarm, and the present scene assumes the added urgency of another one.

Motion pictures become most upsetting when compressing change into a short space, alternating levels of one conflict and combining different forms. Stress is assumed only when presented in primal terms. Close, visible physical danger automatically takes this shape, and it is joined without the slightest preparation. Other conflicts may have to be transformed to make their private concerns public. Not everybody's predicament bothers us, and it has nothing to do with whose it is. Watching a well-liked character become increasingly uncomfortable does not necessarily make the picture any more stressful. We might see him anxiously waiting by the phone and watching the clock, but unless the subject of this possible call is connected to a conflict already inside us, we do not share his state. We wish for the best and know that this now-or-never business deal is of great importance to him, yet, even when we see him becoming more distraught, our body still fails to show much of his agitation. If audience anxiety is intended, any new concern must be cast in terms of the primal equation.

Picture the possible failure to receive a call by showing negative forces acting on the person, and it is a completely different story. It could start with the sound of another bell that takes him to the door and the irritable old lady from next door with more than the same old complaint. This time his dog not only has dug up the flower bed, but also refuses to come out from under her house, and she has come armed with a policeman. Her nonstop harangue makes it increasingly difficult to listen for the phone, and there is no getting away from having to retrieve the dog. Now, for the first time, we share a form of our friend's anxiety. The disturbance is without much independent threat and might be somewhat amusing, but the force is sufficient to physically separate someone from a pressing need. It will create greater distress when the dog refuses to appear even for its owner, responding only with excited barks. The man is now on hands and knees half into the tight crawl space. If we see him through the window from inside his house, and the phone begins to ring, our personal agitation becomes decided alarm. Having become involved in so much of what is seen, we may feel we share all his concerns and overlook that our likeness is restricted to the lines of this presentation. We still do not assume any feeling of his financial pressure for the phone call, but merely share a related experience of being disconnected.

Had the outcome of this awaited call been linked to a conflict previously felt, simply staying by the phone would provide some suspense. Since this concern had yet to be shared, to take us it had to come in a pictured collision of forces. Taking him from the telephone is effective, but there is no shortage of other avenues. The plot might require the communication to occur in person. The spot could be at an airport before the contact must embark, and our friend has been unavoidably detained. His car provides a good vehicle for delivering agitation as well as making us passengers, and its negative movement has two ways to go. Lack of speed forced by unusual traffic and unexpected obstacles tie us to his frustrating disablement and sense of lost cause. Excessive speed can add other anxieties and more sensations of being there. We have yet to acquire the man's motive for the meeting, but traveling too fast or too slow in what will be a close call does activate our partnership. We share a related goal and many connected anxieties. Each reshaping of a character's solitary concern for public consumption sends its own form of distress. It is why we need not even know why a person is pressed to make it on time to experience agitation. We participate only in where the motive leads us, its identity extraneous to suffering the consequences.

We acquire much more of a character's condition when we have been part of the founding conflict. Sequences gain power by connecting to encounters still active within us. The disturbing rush through traffic could be headed for church. The driver has detected unnatural goings-on about town, people not quite themselves with subtle changes in appearance, and he has found a possible connection. Before any changes, the people had been inexplicably drawn from their homes, taken by the feeling that they had to go someplace. He has called to inform his best friend, but the wife said that her husband, without knowing why, suddenly felt some inner calling to visit their church. The danger still makes little sense, but the rush to warn him is a sure emergency. We are caught in a traffic jam, taken too quickly down a side street, narrowly avoiding a close collision, and are even momentarily put in the place of a nearly hit pedestrian. Cut to the friend driving his car with a strange, blank expression. He arrives at the church and heads for the door. Cut back to the first car where we are stopped by a traffic cop who thought he had heard everything. Cut to the church's interior, where we see the friend light a candle, then genuflect and cross himself before taking a seat in front of a woman who remains motionless, head bowed. Cut to the ticketed driver, stalled a bit more before he is allowed to take off. Return to the church. The woman slowly lifts her head, and we see the missing face of onionskin and slits for eyes with a horrifying emptiness that will embrace us all. The sequence will continue to intercut the two characters' developing situations. The two journeys will be ours, and our undoing will be an expanding composite of every seen state.

Films have two ways of framing their flow of events. *Active presentations* employ the terms of engagement, and they are visible forces in immediate opposition. *Passive presentations*, such as anxiously waiting by a silent phone or receiving good or bad news, comprise all other forms of film. Set outside of the equation, these scenes may provide knowledge or even a direct view of events, but they cannot produce profound experience on their own. They must connect to conflicts already formed by the founding factors to strike us. Updates on old disorders will work when passively presented, but, as always, everything is most powerful when arriving in active terms. As experienced in our race to church, more than one individual's reduction can be entered in our personal equation.

Multiple Exposures

Seen in a shot of threatened people, each unique state of standing will make an impression. Our equation, however, cannot multiply a shared position. Two in the same spot are no more than one. Should an intruder with a gun threaten a couple bound back-to-back, our alarm is no more than what would be felt from seeing only one victim, and this remains so should they both be dispatched by a blast of gunfire. Divide and conquer them in different positions within the conflict, however, and a second equation is instantly experienced. If, while one is helpless before the weapon, the other is innocently about to enter the room, our agitation is expanded in scope and size. We equate with what we see, but only shapes of different states register in our reproduction. Properly presented in unfolding situations, however, more than one person enormously enriches the possibilities of our assumed conditions.

The sight of unalike targets within a single shot can create personal disturbance beyond natural experience. We are in the middle of Mardi Gras, where a pair of undercover cops has been attempting to infiltrate a Caribbean smuggling racket. The detective on our side of the street knows they have been set up and that his partner, seen waiting in the crush of the far sidewalk, is about to be shot from an approaching float. Everything is visible in a high-angle wide shot. With three points of interest, a mass of people fills the frame, mostly static, with a narrow strip in motion slowly flowing through it. To get a good look at the parade, the waiting victim makes sure that no one is in front of him, successfully maintaining an open exposure to approaching execution. While we assume the discomfort of the far position, we watch the nearby partner and also share his condition. He must bridge the gap before the float, and he is also in some personal danger. Despite the short distance, the marching band makes shouting pointless, and attempts to cross prove impossible through the passing congestion of drums and horns. The flow advances the elevated threat straight toward its stationary target in a steady, unalterable course. The possible savior must confront it all broadside, and it is all obstructions and delays in a race for life reduced to terrible slow motion.

The scene that remains too close to call is also an unnatural state of affairs where we simultaneously suffer opposite sides of the street. Across the way, passivity in the face of danger is created by a failure to see it. Closer to the camera, a desperate inability to act requires the perception of crisis. We assume two fearful positions that stand on contrary perspectives of innocence and awareness. Mutually exclusive disturbances are experienced through twin targets.

We may have seen this scene before, but new reworkings can still impress us. Framed in the same space, a containment more powerful than intercutting, circumstances unfold exclusively from imagery, and they portray multiple dimensions of our breakdown with directness and economy. The controlling forces, moving and motionless masses, are pure and graphic, heightening our anxieties from the approaching menace, stationary target, and blocked help. Had the distant onboard assassin been seen closely, clown-costumed with a skull face sawed off some victim, the bare bone prettied up with smudged lipstick and blotches of rouge, the threat could also contain chilling suggestions.

Due to its arrangement, this setting for one person's possible demise provides far broader disturbance than some sights for inescapable and wholesale destruction. An island cabin holds some able-bodied fishermen awaiting a tsunami that could take out everything. It is a disturbing sight, but our alarm is unrelated to the number of people to be lost or any differences between them. We look about the place and see individuals reacting in their own ways. Some may even have become our friends. Despite these distinctions, each person's position evokes similar discomfort, and we suffer no more collective anxiety from the group than we do from any one member. The space is confining to occupants and filmmaker. This is a wholly neutralized gathering, and the director is denied the use of elements that will produce more than one equation of altered states. Having characters act differently from one another fails to change their shared condition. Introducing other negative forces to selectively strike some of them would add little weight to the overriding impact we feel from seeing the wave's approach. Every person's standing has the same exposure to the closing swell of destruction.

Bound to the rules for our reactions, the director is unable to compound anxiety with different states. One solution is to enrich his cast of characters. It could be a young child, bewildered and terrified, and a baby blissfully unaware of the inevitable holocaust. Now matters have changed on a most primal level. Both additions seen within the group are instantly distinguished from the rest, and a rush of agitation is added to disturbance. This might appear to be an exception to the audience playing no favorites, possibly protective instincts for the young, but it is no more than our standard formulation. Our concern stems from seeing where they now stand, and it is worse than word of their death. We continue to remain separate from their feelings, finding a close-up of a smiling baby as disturbing as the sight of a tearful child. For us, the infant without awareness and the child lacking strength are conditions of significantly reduced self. As the point and attitude of our experience, they are the least-liked positions when facing disturbance. Even when there is no way out, both strike us with additional and distinct exposures to the scene.

A second solution, decidedly better for developing drama, is to employ the two-wave phenomenon. The first sweep has strewn people all over the island, drowning some while leaving everybody else in all sorts of bad shape. We can now take on a variety of primal impairments even though the surf is up for everybody's wipeout.

There are no exceptions to the rules. The two chatting beside the bomb are no more disturbing than one talking to the other on the phone. A large gathering is identical unless one of its members chooses to settle on top of the chest concealing the explosives. Now our agitation is decidedly elevated, but all from one person. We feel compelled to focus on the most proximate position, and it becomes the sole measure of the same condition. Multiple exposures require pictures of different reductions, not simply separate impressions of a shared state. There are two ways for this to occur, and both are seen at Mardi Gras. By their position in the picture, people face different forces. They may also differ in disabilities, such as immediate awareness, a form of physical incapacity, or, in some films, psychic scars of diminished selfhood. Even if these primal signatures of negative identity do not alter the actual situation, they will be entered in the equation and will color our anxiety with their disturbing character.

Compounding Reductions

Narrative film is a collection of separate situations, and it often leaves people behind while picking up new ones. Fright films, however, create an overriding, continuous story by action and imagery aimed at our insides. Multiple exposures to changing conditions create compounding loss. Simple elements require little craft to make them work, but they dramatically benefit from better employment. Exploiting their potential, even without harm to his characters, Alfred Hitchcock was always able to disable his audience.

In **North by Northwest** (U.S.A., 1959), Hitchcock designed a mountaintop living space with crosscurrents of conflict, connecting figures to multiple forces that constantly change. The home is the site for a scene of high tension. The film's entanglement has centered on a character played by Cary Grant, and it is tied to a disturbing and inexplicable shift in identity. Friends and foes alike mistake him for a mysterious espionage agent. Eventually he will reestablish his own self and secure a safe distance from trouble, but he feels compelled to reenter the situation. Our man has developed strong feelings for a friendly female informant who is acting as the ringleader's mistress, and he is willing to risk his life to separate her from dangerous and distasteful undercover duties.

It is night. The setting is a cliffside, two-level, glass-fronted house over-hanging high on Mount Rushmore, though well below the great stone faces. From outside the brightly lit and wide-windowed complex, Grant has a clear view of both floors. Upstairs, Eva Marie Saint is completing her packing. Downstairs, James Mason and Martin Landau also are preparing for the small plane soon to arrive on a nearby strip. The bi-level home provides unusual openness between floors as well as to the outside. A place where both sides of conflict can be visually connected in the same shot, it is an ideal setting for our altered states. Hitchcock must stick to the primal formula, but he takes it two steps farther. He not only inhabits a third spot in proximate location, but gives all the spots different perspectives on the others. Surely when separated, and even when together, people will not view the same occurrence.

It brings mixed perceptions to existing cross-purposes, compounding the permutations of conflict. Adding to these various viewpoints, events occur that cut both ways, for better and for worse from a single act. Sometimes a few words will instantly alter what we see, but for the most part it is a remarkably visual set of circumstances where even lesser elements of change are graphically told.

For Grant to emerge from the shadows risks making himself visible to both levels of the setting, although his hushed voice would only reach Miss Saint should she step out onto the upper deck. A pebble against the glass goes unnoticed. A second catches her ear. The third promises success as she starts to come out onto the patio. He moves into the light to reveal his presence, but the clatter of the last stone is bringing Landau to the living room window. Withdrawing quickly from sight, Grant luckily avoids detection by the enemy, but the opportunity to become known to his lady is lost. A moment's reduction in tension is replaced by serious alarm, and both shifts are the consequence of a single act. The pattern is soon repeated. As Landau turns from the window to face Mason across the room, we see from outside that he is concealing Miss Saint's small automatic behind his back. Grant sneaks close enough to overhear. Landau is criticizing his boss for having no suspicions of the woman. From our position his manner and movements suggest that he may be about to fire the weapon at his unaware superior. He does, and Mason doubles over in shock before collecting his wits. The gun's blank report is a telling one from Landau: the startling disclosure that the woman and weapon are frauds, and her earlier use of the gun against Grant must have been staged for their benefit. This disturbing discovery requires a change in their plans. She will be dropped from the flight—over water. Just as it appeared that the enemy would be cut in half, potential victims doubled in a flash. From this moment on, every new angle on this developing scene can frame us in two different spots in deepening trouble.

The need to unite our two friends is suddenly tied to heightened agitations, and the couple has become more separated. Grant has entered the home from upstairs, but the marked victim has innocently joined the murder-minded twosome in the living room. He peers helplessly over the edge of the balcony with a full view of the lower level. Miss Saint is seated on the sofa near the two men, and the plane is heard making its first approach. Grant's helpless activity coexists with her blind passivity in a composite portrait of a primal breakdown. Along with mixed viewpoints, new conditions will continue to present themselves. Even within the same frame, friend and foe occupy separate perspectives. One perspective could help them. A second will cause our man's capture.

Seen in the mixed company below, the sight of Grant's monogrammed matchbook would cause only his friend to take notice. With a warning scribbled inside, the matches land unnoticed at her feet. We are suddenly frozen with an added rush of anxiety when the enemy is the one that spots the matches and picks them up, but our alarm soon settles a bit when the message safely ends up in intended hands. This change for the better, however, is soon canceled. The lady must walk with the men to the plane, and her unarmed friend is the only possible source of help. On his way after them, another set of differing perspectives completely transforms the entanglement. A woman working for the other side has remained in the house. She is downstairs, facing away from the balcony, while Grant silently heads for the staircase. Suddenly enemy and audience are struck by imagery from the television's blank screen. The glass reflects a faint impression of the expanse behind her, and we see Grant crossing the landing. We see his perception of safety and her sight of alarm, and it pictures our worst position so far. It is fair warning. We are about to be stopped cold on the stairs by the armed woman.

Hitchcock designed an ideal setting for the peril of his characters, soon to include the stone faces atop the mountain. More importantly, he constructed the place to best frame his audience's inclusion. Its close quarters house the disturbing proximity of figures and threatening forces. Open vistas allow separate sides to be seen together, providing the most visually direct and emotionally powerful connections. Conflicting dimensions are also built into its framework. The complex is all confining isolation as well as threatening exposure, and the unusual layout also creates unalike perspectives for its occupants. Depending upon where they stand, people have unshared lines of sight, and these different visual viewpoints will come with personal ones, differing motives and knowledge. The architect inhabits his space for multiple impact. Two linked, separately endangered people and more than one enemy confront one another from distinct positions of sight and understandings. The permutations of possible conflict are enormously increased by powerful cross-construction.

Given so many compelling angles on conflict, Hitchcock is able to take his best shots. His selection is certain to frame situations in highly visual terms. Figures and forces are directly linked within the picture. Known differences between people's motives are seen in behavior, and understood distinctions in awareness often are visualized by physically different perspectives. Events unfold with little reliance upon words, and significant pieces of dialogue will be reproduced in action. Every critical turning point is founded not only on imagery but on pictures with multiple impact. All will be seen differently by those on screen. Some sights will even strike us with contradictory impressions, switching their meaning with a sudden shift in context. The richness of images, many with mixed dimensions, produces a multitude of equations with all elements provided. Virtually every point in the sequence is an active presentation of at least one assumed condition, and they will take us every step of the way. The picture is also consumed by change, both simple and complex. There are frequent shifts in people's proximity to disturbance as well as distance from their goals, and they continue to produce uncomfortable alterations in our level of anxiety. New angles on action depict different conditions, and pivotal moments reframe every subsequent shot. In a quick succession of events, the stakes are raised and every future state transformed.

Our involvement in the plot is certainly heightened by our great liking for Grant and fondness for Miss Saint. We may look forward to the undoing of Mason's smug duplicity and Landau's brutishness. We might even seek satisfaction from seeing unfairness set right. Many aspects of the story may propel our interest, but the core experience of being there is reduced to the equation. The director operates at this level with distinction. Changing conditions always create the most impact when compressed into a short space. A filmmaker's task is made easy by sequences of wholesale destruction or even suspense when a large number of elements come together. Hitchcock places added burden on his craft by keeping his characters free from harm, avoiding a confusion of too many forces, and refusing to employ crude devices. Despite the director's self-restraint, a great deal happens to the onlooker in a short time. A plain situation is exploited with mixed dimensions of the complex, multiple figures, cross-purposes, distinct perspectives, and double-edged turning points. We may not spot the solidness of this cross-construction, but there is no avoiding the strength of our collapse.

Seated in front of a frightening show, we go many places and follow many people. Somewhere, up there behind us, reels unwind a string of different stories, but for us it will be a singular experience. Our psyche becomes synchronized with the projector in a frame-by-frame reframing of ourselves sprung by automatic mechanisms. This is the overriding story, continuous with the uninterrupted sensation of direct involvement in many places. In the same shot we may be in more than one spot at the same time, suffering different, even contradictory, states. Cut to strangers in unrelated confrontation and we are instantly there, dissolving into our new picture with still-active afterimages. We may even experience fatality, then head downward to a deeper disturbance. As in life, though here more primal, there is constant change, and all things may come together to compound conditions completely. This is our projected picture. Without a break we will be split into a variety of shapes and taken to completion.

VIII. Gut Reactions

We find ourselves impossible to explain. Our intellect continues to prove too feeble to fathom its complexities, and our emotions significantly inhibit their own study by being so squeamish about human experiments. We remain an unpredictable product of countless influences of uncertain importance. Our behavior, however, is a far greater mystery in life than at the movies. In fright films, we will follow a formula of just a few influences, with each one delivered in predictable proportions.

Roots of Response

It begins with biology. Confrontation is perceived, and a few elements compute a level of undifferentiated stress. Within their own environment most animals do the same thing. Factoring import and relative strength, reduced standing is felt. It may add up to no more than easily overcome competition over a minor matter, or as much as an overwhelming attack by a more powerful predator. Dealing with danger, distance is critical. Inside a perimeter of safe distance triggers contact, and stress increases with proximity. The sight of close confrontation activates us, puts us right on the spot, and it is the only conflict to do so. Wired only for such emergencies, bound to present perceptions, we are not under the control of any future concerns, even when these worries are more serious.

By instinct we see what the assailant is saying, and we reply with an inborn response. Their looming body expresses threatening strength, the face tells deeper intent, and its eyes lock it all on us. We automatically recoil from these inherited signs, which in movies and in nature may be amplified, and even seeing something small suddenly inflate is surprisingly disturbing. Puff-uppery anywhere may be a bit overblown, but by no means all bluff, and we better believe it. A meaningful magnifier of actual threat, it is a good indicator of what is behind it, a measure of how this thing compares itself with us.

Confrontation spotted by instinct will be scanned by our psyche. In chillers we will find signs not seen by other animals. Facing us dead-on are expressions of human malice with a malignant combination of our emotions. Seen by our unconscious, they enter an irrational realm where expressions assume insidious dimensions, and symbolic signs may be more troubling than real ones. We feel the danger's dissolution and consumptive negation, and we will see the losing side struck by these designs. Even without schooling we will consider ourselves in existential terms as we assume sensations of being and nothingness.

A piece of biology and part of our mind are the sum and substance of our reaction. Stress from organic jeopardy is compounded by chilling concerns for selfhood, and the punch is a shot of pure adrenaline with a generous dose of deepest dread. This is all there is, even when the last agent is added to the mix.

Here, as in life, reactions will be reshaped by experience, learning by conditioned reflex. Something associated with an earlier stressful scene sends us the same sense of alarm. Stimulus-response education can't be dismissed, and fear is a powerful enhancer of memory. Fright hits the spot that triggers added activity in the hippocampus—the place where fresh inputs are put together and selected for storage—and every aspect of bad experience will be etched into our brains. Learning by association is strict and simple, the way it was in infancy, and learned signals can stimulate every linked sensation in a swell of past emotions. During the course of the picture, predicaments and their agents continue to create new impressions, grow in strength, and compound in character, making new connections while rivetingly repeating old ones. Rules of reinforcement, however, work both ways. To a surprising degree, even the automatic fear of a horrific being can be erased by a small amount of counter-reinforcement, such as seeing the creature relaxing at home or quietly completing a number of ordinary activities. He is no less dangerous, but learning at this level is all that we have come to feel. Monsters should stay on-message.

Based down by our brain stem, deep down in our limbic system, resides the root of all fear, an evolutionary and everyday precursor of thought—a maker of gut reactions and shaper of further understandings. Chillers may stimulate higher intellect, but it will all come down to primitive perceptions. When we put all the facts together and suddenly see what we trusted is anything but safe, the shock of pure deduction is by power of an existing equation. Thought can do no more than identify or redefine active presentations still set in our minds, shaping organic responses but not making them. Intellect is also given little weight, losing out to sensory evidence. Unlikely situations rich in psychic imagery are easily accepted, and any reasoning will be refuted by what we know we are feeling. Although we remain able to judge situations from many angles and choose our own viewpoints, fright films enter our inside with a narrow perspective. Complex conflict is stripped down to a simple picture of naked confrontation. A sparse, prehuman sketch provided by nature is fleshed out with some human expressions and self-conceived symbols of selfhood, and everything else is immaterial until framed in this design.

For all of our individual differences, fear is a great equalizer, reducing us to the same reflexive responses. Horrific movies make us even smaller and more alike by always putting us in the same spot in a surreal world. The whole place is a universe of primal forces, powers fixed to strip away any intruder. When we find ourselves lost at these movies, this is where you'll find us.

Where We Stand (a review)

Our reduced standing is set by what we always see. The horrific chiller is distinguished from all other melodramas by the unique character of its central menace and core events. Both elements evoke immediate experience, and for each it is the sensation of selfhood's dissolution and primal extinction. The enemy instantly explains itself by its appearance, and three simultaneous translations speak directly to emotion. Defining events carry far greater diversity, and the essential elements of their enactment are less apparent. A systematic search for what is always there reveals two pairs of multipliers, plus one addition. The first pair is found in all films of forced tension. The rest is what makes the most disturbing pictures.

The subject matter of every memorable scene and story is always our original conflict, and the whole world taken in is similar to the one first seen. Everything is the shape of sensation perceived with primitive logic. With unsecured boundaries, we must find both safe separation and needed inclusion. Then and now, a breakdown in this balance will erase boundaries and overwhelm us with sensory assault. Events defining the genre always reduce us by isolation and invasion. We enter a universe of no ordinary imagery, where forms are no more than assemblages of unsettling, deeply penetrating signals, and where we are returned to rudimentary responses and understandings.

Along with the illusion of actual involvement, viewers believe that their connection is from worrying about someone. We may have these concerns, but our core condition is independent of caring for victims, their feelings, or anybody's future. The only forced discomfort and deepest disturbance is strictly self-centered and locked to the immediate moment. Figures and forces must meet head-on and on-screen. We will instantly assume the loser's standing, a state of few dimensions. Despite any illusions of feeling otherwise, we follow the form of seeing ourselves in such shape.

The web of present perceptions is a simple snare of sparse construction, a remarkably strong network of linkages that grip us in unbreakable lines. It takes us solely by sight of close confrontation and shakes us more soundly from a small set of primal symbols. This snare has many ways to do this. While tied to present perceptions, we may become connected to the past. Signals associated with earlier upheavals instantly trigger conditioned experience, and we are right back in the hold of old tensions. While we remain bound to the moment, the present may expand within us while standing still on-screen. Continued viewing heightens concern as our eyes dart back and forth between elements in conflict, repeatedly reinforcing their critical links of connection. Our concerns can even change in character in reviews of the scene for more serious suggestions. Symbolic logic may find supporting signs for a surreal reappraisal, and formerly unfelt possibilities become part of the picture.

All moments become new ones, and their captive audience will be consumed by change. Levels of alarm will move up and down, making us more agitated than a steady source of stress. One alarm will lead to another in a string of events, and some events will take on additional feelings by connecting to the course of other ones. And any one of these presentations may alter itself by other associations and psychic meanings.

With additional victims, we may be in more than one entanglement at the same time. Seeing two in the same shape will not alter our impression, but pictures of differing loss strike widening wounds of multiple exposures. A succession of singular and divided states will leave us completely done in and done over.

In our unfolding picture, unshakable situations are woven from sensory associations rather than higher understandings. Conflict in any other shape cannot hold us, and passive presentations must be connected to be felt. Drawn with artful symmetry, craftfully cross-constructed with multiple lines of tension, even lesser elements will create unusual discomfort. The snare's designer, however, need not have Hitchcock's slyness, style, or sophistication to pull the strings. Crude constructions can carry us all the way. And in the end, we may come to the point where we assume all primal signatures. Stripped clean of capacity and personal appearance, a complete victim confronts an altogether destroyer.

PLATE 2

PLATE 3

PLATE 4

PLATE 5

Plate 6

PLATE 7

Plate 8

IX. Birth of the Horrific Being

From the time of its origin in the early years of motion pictures, the horrific chiller has survived as one of film's most powerful and prolific genres, enjoying three major periods of evolution and expansive production. Its classic era of emergence spanned the final decade of silent films and firmly established itself within the new world of sound. Commencing with the fifties and lasting midway through the next decade, the genre enjoyed an unparalleled bloom of production. Feeding upon a fresh and rapidly growing youth market, fright films successfully adapted to new tastes and times, including the industry's climate where low-budget double bills were standard practice for younger audiences. Horrific chillers proved to be particularly well suited to assembly-line production and teenage consumption, and this both stimulated and confined their growth. Scary movies were spawned in unprecedented numbers, but none were free from restrictive financing. Product will follow profit, however, and both would change. It occurred in the mid-seventies with big-budget spending and blockbuster returns, and it produced a third period of expansion that continues today. Now a full-fledged, first-class, mass-market genre, pictures could benefit from all resources of the industry. High finance, state-of-the-art techniques, and more modern conceptions created a new era of resurgence and adaptation.

Throughout its varied evolution the horrific chiller has continued to explore new environments and develop its own form within fresh surroundings. Most films widely found to be the most frightening arrived early in an era of growth. Each of these pictures also gave birth to a singular being, one that still survives as the strongest member of its territory. Universal to the genre, the embodiment has proven remarkably adaptive to changes in industry, marketplace, and world, evolving while maintaining its own identity. Each classic chiller presents a destroyer of novel appearance, yet all of these individuals are essentially the same. Every new creature recasts shared dimensions, and no other salient features will be seen. They are all dissolution and primal aggression drawn from a small set of visual signs. The uniformities are telling. While the being developed to fit diverse settings, it revealed a nature fixed by the immutable mold of our psyche.

Union of Twin Disorders

The Cabinet of Dr. Caligari (Germany, 1919) is the first masterwork of the horrific genre. The film enacts primal conflict within a dreamlike realm, and every part of the being is present. The menace, however, is a pair in a singular alliance, a mad magician and his sleepwalking agent of robbery and murder. The mastermind's shape is twisted with obsessive purpose, and his face bursts with the pleasure of deformed emotions. Mindlessly carrying out doctor's orders, the ashen-faced somnambulist is no more than the missing ingredients of the whole menace. His lean body enclosed in a black leotard, Cesare is all white face and hands, and his dissolute visage is unreflective of what his hands are doing. The film is a wonderfully original chiller and thoroughly universal in its elements. It is also designed to be art. The picture is best remembered by its sharply angled sets and painted backdrops, the distorted landscape of German expressionism. Exaggerated perspectives stretch and squeeze space into unnaturally wide expanses and tight confinements. It is a vision of madness, disorienting and disturbing.

For a movie so absorbing and rich in unsettling imagery, even its first, most easily frightened audiences have found the film to be surprisingly diffuse in its terror. The explanation is not in the elements, but their arrangement. The visual dimensions of the primal menace are all present, but they are split between two beings and reflected with greater force by the environment. Although the destroyer is doubled, and no aspect is lost other than having all designs displayed in one body, this proves to be a poor trade. Even together, the two figures present a less fearsome sight than if their compounding and conflicting qualities were seen within a single person. Their divided image is further diminished by the powerfully surreal landscape, and it is the setting that we most recall rather than its center of destruction. The movie as a whole has all the ingredients, but their placement weakens our perception of focused assault. For the menace, two are less than one by divorcing the dissolute agent of death from the malignant monster that directs it. This setting is also too much and set out in the wrong direction, failing to merely echo the danger at a distance, resonating diminishing tremors from its living epicenter.

The horrific being was born out of a union of dual disorders, the dark forces of selfhood's dissolution and primal extinction. It became the singular embodiment of horrific experience, its unique form no more than some universal signals set to assault our psyche. *Caligari* most memorably marks its origin. The twins had yet to join into one that becomes the center of less powerful surroundings, and we feel more disoriented than directly aimed at our undoing. The genre's first extraordinary example combines all of the imagery and action within one picture. In every classic to follow, ingredients would come together to take us apart by assuming the shape of a most singular being.

Original Creations of Shared Dimensions

The emergence of a new genre heralded one-and-a-half decades of remarkable growth, and every form it took featured a unique creature that boldly displayed the dimensions of our two most feared departures. Both *Nosferatu* (Germany, 1921) and *Dracula* (U.S.A., 1931) were based upon Bram Stoker's popular gothic novel and his chillingly envisioned vampire. This being survives today as the classic supernaturally formed menace, reappearing more than any other character in the movies. The silent, foreign version was unauthorized, altering much of the original story to circumvent copyright. Although structure and plot were weakened, the image of Count Orlok was hauntingly horrific. Here and in Werner Herzog's visually powerful remake (Germany, 1976), a man drained of life has become ratlike in the process. Decay is seen in a skeletal head of pale skin, eyes sunken into their dark surrounds, lost hair, and bony hands. Added to his losses are animalistic features. A centered pair of fangs overhangs large, dark lips, elongated fingernails are curled to claw, and big angular ears flare forward. Nosferatu is an alarmingly loathsome sight. Trim in a tight, dark, well-worn overcoat, with a bit of affectation this degenerate may even strike the pose of a jaunty gentleman, an insidiously infectious look made more unnerving by being so intangibly unsettling.

With what was an individual wasted away, and parts of predator assumed, Count Orlok is pure dissolution and extinction. Count Dracula has a far less fearsome and bestial appearance, but the dimensions are identical. Ashen with fangs, lifeless and bloodthirsty, Dracula visually describes both his eroded identity and annihilating replacement. Quite by accident, it came with a voice that oddly amplifies these qualities. A star suddenly stricken was a lucky break for Lugosi, and casting went from one of the screen's most gifted performers to a ham actor who had overplayed the part on stage. His courtly and alien Hungarian accent and stylized histrionics turned out to work, and by his voice Bela became the singular and lasting prototype. The rhythms and emotional distance are sternly polite, slow to react, and suggestive of a driven creature, passionless even in absolute obsession. This state is shared by both counts, and it comes possessed with dreadful powers—the dissolution of our free will in the hypnotic spell of seduction, and the primal extinction of our old identity by sucking out some of our blood. More horrific than injury or death, this thing will leave us alive while taking us all away.

Before we become prey to its inhabitant, a towering realm confronts us, looming oppressively above us with unsettling suggestions. Outsiders who enter will shortly sense their anonymity. Although who they are and why they are there differ in the many movie versions, it is soon clear that this has no meaning to their host or to their future. The particular appearance of the vampire also varies, but it need not enact its malevolent motives to make us feel a related dissolution. The loss of self is reflected in its face as well as what we see in the looking glass. Annihilation will also become unmistakable when the entity chooses to reveal itself completely, and it will be from the primal posture. Whether alighting upon a sleeping victim or suddenly looming up over a seated guest, its grimacing fangs threaten from above.

Prior to the most memorable creature of supernatural creation, the most frighteningly featured individual of natural origin had already arrived out of the silent screen, and it was also a portrait of pure dissolution and primal aggression. In the remarkable *The Phantom of the Opera* (U.S.A., 1925), the fiend is no more than the universal menace, but its features are arranged in a most grotesque and immediately informative manner. Lon Chaney's living skull possibly says it all more than any other horrific visage. It is all out front. Lost to fire, the outer layer of face is gone, leaving pale tissue tight against bone. Although his eyes bulge with intensity, they appear to have receded deep into their sockets. What is left of the nose is peaked and pushed up, prominently displaying a pair of big black holes. Surrounding skin has pulled away from the mouth, revealing rotting and separated teeth, and this fixed snarl is surely bestial. When the stretched lips are tightened further, they form the smile of enraptured evil.

Grandiose, narcissistic, and swollen with self-serving alienation and contempt, the phantom is able to find pleasure within his victimized and love-lost existence. Unlike the hapless vampire forced to follow some unearthly duty, at best enjoying a moment's passion, the fiend is fueled by desires of his own selection. He bursts with an unnatural mix of emotions, thriving on the thrill of unchecked human appetites, while advertising his lost humanity with the stripping away of facial features and by exposing the creature at its core. For the vampire, it is unnatural transmutation, not inner revelation, and the process is well expressed by the draining of life inside coupled with bestial additions. Fiend and vampire are instantly recognized as distinct individuals. We see what made them, what they want, and what's in store for us. Despite dissimilarities, they are very much the same. Differing designs of shared dimensions describe their own ways of dismantling us and taking our entirety.

Both individuals arrived from a setting yet to produce a classic creature, and both became its master. Though assuming a new shape that displayed their own nature, they were also no more than newborn bodies of shared identity. The signatures are seen again in the remaining great success of the chiller's early era, *Frankenstein* (U.S.A., 1931). The film also centers on a humanlike being. This time the beast was a product of earthly science fiction, fantasy free of the beyond, and it survives as the foremost and most often reappearing figure of its origin. The creature's appearance presents a fresh form, but it is no more than dissolution and annihilation, pure and primal. Assembled from anonymous corpses without assuming a personal name, mature personality or intellect, it gains the power to dismember and destroy. Visually this was best realized in the original silent Edison short (U.S.A., 1910). Only stills remain, but even these are more disturbing than the existing moving and audible monster. This earlier one is a rotting, misshapen assemblage of body parts and tattered clothing. The face is unnaturally small and slightly misplaced within this malformed amalgamation. Were it not for its deathly pallor, it might become lost within the dark, oversize head and tangled surround of overgrown hair. Deep-set eyes are mismatched, the mouth no more than a deformed cavity. Surely it is the specter of decay and nonidentity, and primal extinction as well. The twisted expression gives fair warning of what the bony hands and clawlike fingers will do.

The classic sound version somewhat sanitized the creature, but it proved most fearsome to audiences of its day. Makeup artist Jack Pierce, with director James Whale, created a strikingly original and powerful embodiment, one that nicely appealed to reason and to its suspension. Reflecting existing technology in medical science, the raised forehead was squared off and flat-topped for the brain's insertion. Bold surgical scars cut across the forehead and upper neck, and clamps secured skull to spine. We accept the possibility of the procedure without wondering why the result is so big. Cast for his height, once well-known players proved unavailable, Boris Karloff was given a widened girth and elevated at the top and from below. The heavy, lumbering gate with arms outstretched and primitive face is all menace.

The getup, one taking a good half day to get on and get off, included an innovation in flexible makeup. Unfrozen facial features allowed for an unusual range of expressed emotions, and the freedom was employed to reveal increasing humanity in a performance that becomes touching, even tragic. Normally good qualities are a bad idea. Any redeeming emotions make the menace much less of a monster and significantly shrink its psychic standing. Facial expressions best remain frozen— sending that awful feeling we get when seeing something that fails to respond to our reactions—or suddenly shift to a more ghastly expression. Here sympathy makes the story stronger, and helping to compensate for the creature's softened nature, we will remain justifiably concerned that out of ignorance or fright, it still could do terrible harm to the nicest, defenseless people.

With the stiff, slow swing of each solid step, unrelentingness is unmistakable. Looming over us with extended arms, reducing us more with a display of disturbingly mechanical postures and expressions, somnambulist, phantom, counts Orlok and Dracula also greet their victims. If their melted faces allow us to wax descriptive, it is not due to their lack of form or to the free flow of our imaginations. Each visage has solidified, reworking and recasting common elements into a fresh shape of pure dissolution and consumption. This early era of the classic chiller produced a number of dissimilar and alike individuals that still live as the model of their personal origin.

Lesser Mutants and Clones

Following its time of emergence and powerful development, one passing into the new era of sound, the horrific chiller failed to evolve further for nearly two decades. Production dwindled in Europe, while America became overpopulated with routine remakes and commonplace creatures.

The loss is reflected in two generations of stars. Lon Chaney was the premier performer of the original era. Born of deaf-mute parents, he brought an early practice of pantomime to his later mastery of makeup. The man of a thousand faces, disguises that always concealed his given appearance and were sometimes grotesque, was not a maker of masks. He was a revealer who, with remarkably telling expressions and compelling physical features, even when these two looks contradicted, unveiled inner essence to our eyes. From the unredeemable hate of the phantom to the noble heart of the horribly deformed hunchback, words were unnecessary with so much expressive behavior. The actor spoke only in one film, and that in the last year of his life. Chaney was favored for his first supernatural role, the bloodthirsty Count of the genre's first talking classic. A malignant throat tumor, said to be the result of his self-devised makeup, soon took his voice, delivering him to the speechless state of his parents and public personas. He died that year, 1930, at the age of forty-seven.

The grand opening of the chiller's first era would be coming to a close. Hollywood recycled its resources, including the memory of the great performer. Creighton Chaney was renamed Lon Chaney Jr. and soon the "junior" was dropped. The son, unfortunately, bore no other resemblance to his father. He was always himself here, overweight and overwrought, appearing to become more and more uncomfortable in his increasingly silly situations and movies.

Many chillers of this period had the same menace return within similar circumstances, and no picture was as strong as the original. Sometimes the creature was resurrected within more modern times without a primitive setting. Dracula appeared unsupported by his archaic domain, and generations of Frankensteins and new monsters would move into more contemporary and civilized surroundings. Most of the remaining examples also featured a humanlike being, but no memorable newcomers were introduced. Along with the absence of overwhelming and original pictures came an abundance of dull and derivative destroyers, old menaces returning in a less primal form. Frankenstein's creature was reduced and recast into the mummy. This single-person resurrection, a body-wrap with badly wrinkled head, was justifiably given little screen time in a chiller surprisingly short on thrills. The supernatural agent of lost self seen in the vampire was turned into the wolf man, too much theatrical victim and too little terrible villain. Evolution was on hold, and no powerful prototype was born or strengthened.

There are very few pictures in any genre where sequels or remakes stand up to a strong original, and the task is even harder for chillers, and superior conceptions are required with the reappearances of familiar monsters. With no fresh crop of formidable creatures, the more evocative new pictures explored the setting. In films, such as the Val Lewton production *Cat People* (U.S.A., 1942), the first creature film to leave the thing unseen, defenseless people find themselves isolated in places of possible danger, places with disturbing shapes and shadows. Mood and suspense was rich and real, and no more was needed for compelling pictures. For horror, however, while uninspired films depended too much on the monster, the rare disquieting film removed too much of it. Not one brought everything together within the overall framework of a lasting totalistic fright film. Successful reproductions of the genre require virgin territories for newborn creatures. The creation of a complete and original classic would have to await a renewal of resources.

X. Resurgence

The fifties arrived with a new marketplace, and it fueled a bloom of production lasting one-and-one-half decades. Although the resurgence of horrific pictures was worldwide, most of these movies and strongest examples were made in the U.S. The genre evolved within an American environment, and ongoing practices in the film industry shaped every creation. Existing black-and-white B-picture assembly lines propagated product, and it was well suited to double-bills and the tastes and tolerances of teenage audiences. The young were voracious consumers, unusually accepting of quickly conceived and poorly nurtured pictures. Many of the weakest films were financially successful, though doomed to the limited life of presold playdates sure to include drive-ins. Some were even financed and readied for photography with only a marketable title, giving just enough time to come up with a story and dash off a script.

Consigned to a low-budget, formula category, fright films were made in a rush with minimal funding for all departments. The vast majority advertises their humble origin, and none escape flaws that stem from financing. They all, however, proved their adaptability to restrictive budgets. Many delivered the whole experience, and a few would be overpowering.

Reproduction and diversity are key to evolution, and the fifties brought opportunity for both. Along with providing the resources for far bigger numbers, the era opened new settings for the genre's development. With unexplained sightings, the eyes of the world were turned to the skies, an unexplored universe for chillers. Postwar film audiences were also more open to darker understandings of human nature. It was a time of new horizons in outer space and the inner mind, and they became the birthplace of the period's two most distinguished fright films. Living at their center was a primal being of fresh form. The most disturbing B-picture created the ultimate terror from another planet, and the class-A masterwork presented the premier psychotic annihilator. Both embodiments were all brand new, but they also brought the old monster back, now reshaped for an unclaimed domain. No less classic than their ancestors, they still dominate their territory.

Pure Progeny, Unique Descendants

Frontiers of science provided the period's most fertile spawning grounds. Atomic testing in the movies released primeval creatures from the bowels of the earth and created gigantic mutants on the surface. It failed, however, to produce any memorable monsters or craft a picture with more than moments of fright. Life from other worlds was prolific and more powerful, bringing a timely menace that could assume the psychic shape of our dehumanized destroyer. It was the titled star of the prime contender for the era's B-picture classic, **The Thing** (U.S.A., 1951). An early and effective confrontation with an outsider, the Howard Hawks production freezes us within its barren, icebound setting, slowly exposing us to the thaw of a humanlike hulk with terribly dissolute features. For completeness of the horrific experience throughout a whole picture, however, it was surpassed by Don Siegel's **Invasion of the Body Snatchers** (U.S.A., 1956). The film is overwhelming, and its intruders arrive in a most primitive form.

Alien seeds drifting through space have fallen to Earth, landing unnoticed in a small town in America. They produce plants with large seedpods that can assume the appearance and knowledge of individual humans. Anyone who sleeps near a waiting pod will be drained of existence. The dormant receptacle begins to develop its delivery—a featureless form within its folds, now metamorphosing into some emerging person, soon to show the face of a sleeping victim. The copied individual will be replaced by the new shell, a look-alike lacking the lost self's personality and emotion. Although the clones may pass for those taken, their expressionless faces and passive movements tell of beings void of their own feelings and any personal identity. They are no more than a shared single purpose. For the good of inferior human beings, including former friends who feel otherwise, it is their manifest destiny to aid the supplanting process. Every person is to be recast into this supreme state of obsessive servitude. We become our own destroyers in the consumption of selfhood.

The influx of alien arrivals typically took another form. They came in flying saucers, and most of them followed one of two tactics. If the craft landed unseen in an underpopulated part of the Midwest, its passenger was a primitive creature who has a grotesque face with all of our features. If the saucer set down near an urban setting, humanoids of high intellect would have slit-eyed, smooth faces void of human individuality and expressive change. Both types are instantly recognized as life from other worlds as well as forms of the universal menace. There was no need for either one to conceal its identity. The primitive variety silently stalks isolated victims and is difficult to stop by conventional means, including army artillery. The civilized embodiment publicly announces its purpose and is already in charge. The body snatchers are among the rare exceptions, and their unique nature places added burden on their author. While the plot requires invisible infiltration, our psyche demands seeing the true face of its invader. It is not enough to know the mission or even see it performed. The ultimate menace must display our twin terrors within its own form. Audiences and townspeople must see things completely differently, and the film successfully serves both ends.

The invaders mature through distinct morphological stages, their early phases privy only to us. Seeds become plants with pods that develop at any location within range of a reproducible form. Wrapped inside, soft protoplasm assuming shape is a terribly disturbing sight, its pale, human face made even more dissolute veiled by the fabric of its cocoon. Completing its picture, this dissolution is turning into us and will be there to be seen in the plant's next and final stage. All individual replacements share signs of our common loss. Their movements are slightly slowed, the speech tones flat, and emotional expressiveness is disturbingly absent, and dangerous, depersonalized traits will be spotted. Despite a near normal appearance, seen in its present context, along with the impressions of its earlier phase, the horrific being is in full view. These embodiments are also part of a remarkably primal experience, for us focusing on a single protagonist and his terrifying discovery, too awesome and too late to reverse. A number of townspeople and some of the authorities already have been replaced. Soon gone will be his neighbors, then an inner circle of confidants, and finally his lover lost to an irrevocable closure of consumption. The sight of collective clones slowly and single-mindedly coming in his direction is a totalistic vision of the primal destroyer, and our terror is of the first order.

The little film enjoyed wide attention. Many film analysts discerned social commentary. Some spotted a denouncement of big-brother regimes overseas, while others were certain of seeing a frightening metaphor for postwar conformity right here at home. Even if the film had some subtext or sensibilities, gratuitous redeeming values did not detract from the art of pure escapism. Analysts and audiences alike agreed upon the power of its only important message, and everyone took it the same way.

Although many of the imperfections common to low-budget pictures are evident, the film's perfect premise, tight construction, and totalism produced one of the finest examples of the genre. The era's other overpowering classic, ***Psycho*** (U.S.A., 1960), was also fashioned from restrictive financing. Even Hitchcock's bankable status did not outweigh the horror film's second-class standing, and he was required to work within an unusually modest budget. The director allocated his resources wisely. While nearly all of the film was swiftly shot, adopting the techniques and speed of shooting a TV show, one scene was crafted at the painstaking pace of an expensive commercial. Seven days were spent at one spot photographing a forty-five-second sequence with seventy setups. The scene brought life to the horrific being and annihilation to its first victim, and its command of imagery would be felt throughout the whole picture. With so much resting on the shoulders of a character restricted to sudden, short, well-spaced appearances, a powerful creation had to be formed from our first impression.

The setting for assault is an overgrown, secluded piece of property, now isolated by a new highway. The maniac resides within an old house, Victorian gingerbread made gothic, standing on a rise behind a low, flat line of run-down motel rooms. The creepy, elevated dwelling provides a sense of dread about its unseen occupant, who, once seen, will fill every room with the aura of horrific presence. An unforgettable first appearance with a butcher's knife cuts short the shower of the motel's only guest. Although the scene is an assembly of flashing close-ups aimed mostly at the woman under attack, we are left with a riveting impression of the assailant. Through the plastic curtain we see the approaching form of an old lady with elevated, oversize blade. Bursting upon the scene, striking from above, the primal intruder performs its frenzied assault and is gone. The blindly repetitive downward blows suggest a primitive reflexive fury. It is a portrait of aberrant and absolute obsession, and it comes with instant dissolution before extinction. Stripping people of a piece of selfhood before tearing apart their body, the lunatic's attack on the woman first rips away the veil protecting her personal space, nakedly exposing her to the outside world. The remaining victim, in a shocking assault on personal appearance, is stabbed once in the face, awaiting a backward trip down the staircase before deathblows are delivered. There is no separating the creature's portrait from its consequences. From a composite of frenzied imagery, a complete form of the horrific being is constructed.

The making of the menace carried a constraint; the audience's unquestioned misreading of the killer's identity. Nicely not calling our attention to the omission, the camera avoids revealing the attacker's face during the second strike by employing an overhead angle from the ceiling. Such a device, however, is unsuitable for our first sighting. Shooting from above diminishes what we see, and it is no way to introduce a primal form. Destroyers assume power by their elevation over us and becoming bigger in our eyes with their approach. Moreover, avoiding the face by any means robs the being of its full potential. This critical first appearance demands construction as well as concealment, and Hitchcock makes the most of it. In shadowy silhouette blurred by the curtain, a face is seen, and it is dark and desolate. This indelible first impression is carried to the end, and when we finally get a better look, coming with the stunning discovery of its terribly twisted nature, we will be startled by how pitiful the terror actually appears. The plastic curtain adds threatening images of dissolution to both sides of the encounter. Immediately after its smooth erasure of humanity from the assailant's face, it unveils a terrifying picture of the victim's loss when her protective boundary is ripped aside. The same piece of scenery also has other uses. It hides who the killer is, and—pop, pop, pop—graphically conveys the weight of the woman's collapse when ripping away from its hangers. The scene is well served. In the bare setting of a bath, as well as any good sequence, its few fixtures are best installed for multiple functions.

It is also possible that positioning plays a part in our disturbance. Danger may be more dreadful when placed to the left. If you recall a few horrific films, ones with an unusually unsettling entrance into the scene, you may find that in most, if not all, the assailant arrives from our left side. In this film's three key establishing shots—the house with motel, Norman peeking through the peep-hole, and the detective on his way to what we see of the second floor—in every shot, the seen or unseen dread is to the left. Flip these pictures to their mirror image, and you are likely to feel that danger has become a bit less sinister. For reasons unclear, it would appear that monsters are well-advised to reside on the left.

And here there is also the music—Bernard Herrmann's highly original and much imitated primal scream of violins, dissonant in its strident bursts of jarring discords as well as with every sentiment associated with the string instrument. The sound is the pure sensation of terror, the most horrific accompaniment to any movie menace. Nearly all chillers contain music that adds to an uneasy atmosphere and warns of impending climax. Some themes, such as the unrelenting bass beat in *Jaws,* are even suggestive of the menace's stalking. *Psycho*'s score, however, was unique. Its keynotes appeared only in the sudden, short periods of on-screen assault, and they well characterize the assailant. What we hear may double for the victim, but the frenzied pulse of piercing shrieks is our vision of the agent. Never employed for suspense, and always exploding from the creature's fury, this is no overture for danger or instrumental theme. It is a surreal sound effect, a vocal signature of the berserk predator, and it becomes a physical part of its identity. The picture of the menace is complete. Supported by its setting, shaped by its action, embodied in its form and left position, and amplified by its cry, a horrifically whole primal being is born.

Hitchcock presented film's most frightening pathological annihilator. Siegel exposed us to the most disturbing alien consumers on Earth. These obsessive agents of their own negation appeared in the era's best-remembered and most continually successful classics. There were, of course, other powerful shockers, including one featuring the other side of madness, assault by terrors of our own making. Although Roman Polanski's *Repulsion* (Great Britain, 1965) never received mass-market distribution in the U.S., and its impact is unrealized on television, many who saw it in theaters found it to be film's most frightening depiction of a crumbling mind. While becoming increasingly disturbed by her sister's live-in lover, the night sounds and daytime reminders of intimacy, a young woman is slipping away from reality. When she is left alone, her fears and fascinations will be actualized in paranoid fantasy.

Nearly half of the movie is uneventful, with little dialogue, but we become immersed in her point of view. More and more withdrawn, she is preoccupied by details that might have escaped our attention, the boyfriend's straight razor left in the drinking glass, a dust spot on a wooden chair, and a widely branching crack in a cement sidewalk. Finding her barricaded by herself in the flat, we sense a growing atmosphere of decay about the place. Curled up and assuming the appearance of an aborted fetus, an uneaten, skinned rabbit lies rotting on a plate, later seen with the razor alongside. We also share the stillness and solitude, and our ears become tuned to the silence and the sharp clarity of a dripping faucet and buzzing fly. All of this conditioning will prove essential to our undoing.

Our fright begins with an explosive jolt of sound alike the shearing of an iceberg, and she turns to see a jagged hairline crack in the plaster extending from an air vent. We are shaken, and the startling sound invests ordinary imagery with unusual power. Later, as she uses a wall switch to light a darkened room, we are hit again by the same sound, and the wall rips apart, exposing a gaping, horizontal break. We are now struck by primal alarm. Previously her concerns were somewhat passively presented. Seeing her frozen by a crack in the sidewalk may suggest her fear of injury or imperfection, or even symbolize the fracture of her mind, but there is no proximate danger. Now entering the confrontational equation as a threatening disturbance, the imagery activates our participation in shared conflict. Her fears become ours, and, as the wall tears apart, the very bottom may be dropping out from under us.

Suffering her madness awaited our model of alarm, and primal signatures make it more disturbing, but not until the signatures take human form does experience become horrific. It is a man first seen in a shocking flash of reflection as she shuts a mirrored door. Coming with powerful jolts of sound, a physically felt bass rumble and the tremble of atonal high notes, it lifts us from our seats. That night, when she is in bed, there are footsteps in the hallway. They come closer, slowing and stopping near her door before continuing down the hall. The next night he is back, there is more stealth to the step, and he is undeniably drawn to the bedroom. The still silhouette of a foot is seen through a crack beneath the door before it silently withdraws. Our suspicion that the intruder is only imagined provides no feeling of relief, and it carries the odious sensation of something both more and less than human. He will not be stopped and even chooses to come through the entrance that she has barricaded. The door opens slightly, hitting the highboy, and she recoils. It strikes again, sliding the furniture a few inches, revealing a vertical slice of the man, sullen and inexpressive. She gasps in terror, but there is no sound other than the loud twice-a-second ticking of her clock. In a series of short close-ups, made more dreamlike by the silence of the action and more frantic by the tempo of the timepiece, we see him in the room and upon her, raping his terrified victim in a passionless, mechanical manner. He will appear another night, suddenly arising beside her from underneath the bedclothes, wholly overcoming her in his silent assault. Other visions of consumption will scare us, and she will be driven to bloody murder, but the horrific core experience remains with the surreal assailant.

Polanski is an unusually gifted craftsman of tensions and their uncomfortable, sometimes perverse, textures, employing simple elements of highly evocative design. The film is remarkable for creating so much fear from, at least by today's standards, so much restraint. Its success derives in part from the slow development. Having absorbed us in her fixations as well as the quiet isolation of her surroundings, the director builds upon our conditioned perspectives by both construction and demolition. New visions are born out of imagery already developed, and they will destroy the established stillness and solitude. Without even the warning of ominous music, the silence is shockingly shattered, and she is not alone. Skill, however, does not free a filmmaker from the formula. We share her terrors only after they have been framed within the equation. The well-chosen images, elemental and graphic, are primal signatures of assault and disintegration, and the dissolution of selfhood is the central subject. To assume their most horrific form, terrors took human shape. Although the man is not seen clearly enough to identify in another setting, we recognize the horrific being. Frightening us with his footsteps or by appearing silently without warning, this featureless and unfeeling dissolute specter is the unstoppable agent of primal assault.

In the related category of frightening dream states, the most commercially successful example is a series of films born twenty years later. On the other side of subtlety and solid construction, *A Nightmare on Elm Street* (U.S.A., 1984–89) intentionally assumes a style of comic book overkill. A surreal slasher with a bloody bag of tricks invades the dreams and lives of teenagers. Although there are some effective moments and imaginative special effects, it is all shock with a lot more splatter than story. The mix of dreams and reality is not designed to condition a more disturbing perspective, but employed to allow as much mayhem as possible without plotted motivation. At the center of the series is the homicidal intruder in our minds, Freddy Krueger. His demonic face and stiletto fingernails instantly identify Freddy as the horrific being, while his rakish hat and gallows humor mark him as a campy cousin. Whether it is these over-the-top nonstop nightmares or Polanski's slowly developed hallucinations, or any example in between, terrifying dreamscapes will be inhabited by the being.

The midcentury period of expansion also introduced a new mode of production to the genre. Three-dimensional pictures enjoyed a short burst of life before many problems took their toll. Producers, predicting quickly fading interest in the process, rushed hastily conceived and poorly crafted product to the screen, and directors usually employed the added dimension to propel objects into the audience rather than deepen the picture's dark vision. The form soon vanished, having produced only one worthwhile shocker. This successful example continues to return in both flat and full projection, surviving along with its memorable embodiment of the primal being.

Although **House of Wax** (U.S.A., 1953) was intended to be good fun, it took the job seriously. The 3-D fright film is more than the best of a poor lot. As a good old horror show, enjoyable for its rendering of all the melodramatic conventions, this is a compelling classic. Reworking **The Mystery of the Wax Museum** (U.S.A., 1933), the plot centers on selfhood, and it could not be more primal. A fire that melts a collection of lifelike figures leaves their creator misshapen in mind and body, now unable to perform his craft without taking artistic license. A new collection is mounted, this time by dipping human bodies in molten wax, restoring the sculptor's lost self by taking and recasting other individuals. Personal disappearance is felt throughout the film and stunningly presented in the two most disturbing pieces of imagery. The first comes in a quick succession of pictures that appear from the fire that sets the story going. While the wax figures melt, we are struck by a series of sensations akin to witnessing the whole process of self's extinction. We feel the loss of individuality as faces begin to erode into pale lumps of forgone features. Seen again, they are awash with a dreadful void of vacant humanity. Suddenly, we are jolted further as the eyeballs fall away inside the skull. Looking into the gaping sockets and dropped jaw, the sight of total emptiness inside is unexpectedly horrific. In fact, all of this is surprisingly disturbing for the demise of lifeless objects. In three successive shots, we watch dissolution, deformed nature, and the absence of all inner being. A moment later, the sight will be primal consumption as the figures vanish forever in the ferment of their own fire.

The most awesome sight is saved for last, once again a reproduction of the picture's theme in a powerful portrait of personal erasure. This time, however, the subject is the horrific being. Some of the more frightening situations have included a hunched-over, twisted-limbed character bent on collecting corpses, creating some more, and stalking the heroine. Dragging one leg, this dark creeper in black cape and wide-brimmed fedora displays his aberrant obsession even in distant pursuit. Seen close up with his face revealed, the sight is horrifying. It is the hideous phantom with a repulsive difference. The outer skin is not simply burnt off, but grotesquely colored, reformed, and scarred. Throughout the film we have been misled into making two characters out of one. We see Vincent Price as the crippled sculptor confined to a wheelchair but otherwise whole, energetically directing apprentices in his perverse project. We view the horrific embodiment as some fiendish aide until the unforgettable climax. Price has designs on the heroine's appearance, and he finally has her in his reach. He suddenly rises out of his chair to take possession. Flailing against his face, the poor woman unveils a terrifying spectacle. What was the man breaks away, a mask of wax covering the melted visage of the monster. The fire that took his face and fingers left only the passion, deformed. Beneath a lifeless copy of former self is a visceral portrait of his true remains. The revelation is shocking, and it extends far beyond the particulars of plot. The dreadful manner by which the external face cracks and crumbles into inanimate pieces, exposing grotesque inner tissue, is one of the most independently powerful images of the era.

The deformed figure maker is more derivative than the original creatures within the era's two outstanding classics. Similar to the star of every successful horrific chiller, however, he is a remarkable individual embodying all the elements of his ancestors. Although other effective pictures continued to appear for a time, the genre would suffer a second period of decline. By the mid-sixties, the population was weakened by too many generations of inbreeding with too little searching for new creations. More people making use of their free screens at home also diminished the marketplace. For the first time, an ultra-low-budget independent horror film enjoyed lasting commercial success. George Romero's *Night of the Living Dead* (U.S.A., 1968) attained a deserved cult following that continues today. Crudely crafted and amateurishly acted, its gruesome presentation takes the tone of a hardcore comic book. Every recently buried body unearths itself, roaming the countryside as a stumbling, seemingly unstoppable, flesh-eating zombie. The picture focuses on a dwindling band of barricaded people surrounded by a gathering parade of hungry corpses. Despite having the appearance of an elaborate home movie, it is unusually frightening. By the power of decomposing and devouring beings, the picture gives life to primal dissolution and primitive consumption and more than survives its bare-bones production. The film stands in sharp contrast to the genre's next stage, however, as the era of minimal financing ended.

XI. Modern Embodiments

By the early seventies, conditions were becoming more favorable for another renewal of terrifying pictures, this time with complete backing of the industry. Scary books were doing well, and some tales of the supernatural had become best sellers. People were also returning to the movies, and blockbuster hits in other genres were increasingly common. Most major successes were big-budget productions requiring far greater financing than had ever been risked on a horror film. The gamble was taken, however, and it paid off with unprecedented profits. Handsomely mounted, grand-scale shockers became commonplace. Even films targeted at teenagers received more than minimum financing, achieving some degree of slickness in style and special effects. More important than improved appearances, conceptions requiring greater expense could now be brought to the screen. For a genre that remains strong only by developing new grounds, this was an opportunity for growth. Fresh forms appeared, but with mixed results. Just as restrictive funding did not prevent the crafting of powerful pictures, unlimited financing would not necessarily make them better.

Mass-Market Monsters

One unusually popular book had the following to hedge a high-stakes blind bet, and **The Exorcist** (U.S.A., 1973) became the first big-budget horror movie. Promoted by an advertising campaign more expensive than the entire cost of making any previous shocker, the film enjoyed returns that beat the past record holder by more than tenfold. Seen by so many people, it is often selected as the all-time scariest film, surely the favorite example of a satanic nature. The little girl lost certainly is a terrible sight, and along with the frightening face and spooky idea, the picture comes with the trimmings of first-class production. Rounded characters are professionally performed. Complex camera setups, lavish lighting, and detailed art direction exhibit finesse, and a wide variety of special effects are state-of-the-art without any trace of artifice.

Despite its popularity and craftsmanship, the picture fails to be a satisfactory classic. A sizable portion of moviegoers agreed with most of the critics, finding the film to be a sensationalistic hodgepodge, repellent without being deeply disturbing. Even its most ardent fans are hard-pressed to recall any prolonged periods of tension or terror. Shocking moments of ghastly expressions and startling effects are well remembered, often along with the troubling belief that much of this actually happened, but the experience of being a victim is lacking. We are impressed by how realistically the girl's head makes a complete revolution and repelled by her bilious expectorations, but this spit-and-polished production is surprisingly short on our sustained participation.

The absence of profound experience was predetermined by the equation of altered states. Identifying with a possessed victim, the loss of power, inner self, and outer appearance is horrifically primal, but this does not happen here. Too soon seeing a monster sending signals of the enemy, we are spared the girl's terrifying consumption by surreal powers. In our equated experience she is the assailant, the priests are the victims, and both parts of the equation fail to be complete. Knowing the risk and free to leave, professionals well armed with powerful icons and incantations approach a bedded menace by their own choice. Willing and aware adversaries seeking battle, even if outmatched, do not occupy the horrific position of ordinary, helpless innocents, chosen targets for consumption. So long as they retain this elevated attitude, every fearsome element entered into the equation will be eased. The other side of confrontation is also softened. The being comes with the right look and sound, but its assault is incomplete in primal behavior. People are never stalked, chased, come upon without warning, or held against their will. The first stage of attack is limited to foulmouthed mind games and beside-the-point magic tricks. The devil does know all about everyone in its presence and will come to play on their weaknesses. This is a good start on selfhood's diminishment, and some crippling concerns are well visualized, but most internal turmoils are not pictured and remain outside the viewer's participation. What we see best, and what proves to be the most dangerous, are physical assaults short on primal signatures. Being hit by flying objects or blown out a window can be fatal, but it is not what we see in the little girl's face or most deeply fear.

The book was based on actual events, though not the amazing ones all made up. Truth went out the window long before the priest. Free to make his own adaptation, the director chose the wrong authority, religiously following the written word rather than the rules that put us squarely in the picture. We should witness more primal loss, and it should take the form of the being's design. The monster's magical ability to rise from the bed is impressive, but even normal movement used to entrap innocents in its aura would have been horrific. If the girl were free to roam when others sleep, visiting those who would liberate her, slowly gaining power while they lie in their reduced state, we would have suffered a terrifying sense of helplessness and surreal disintegration. There are many ways to portray the malignant, invasive nature of satanic forces, and all are far more frightful than spirited one-upmanship between well-armed agents of good and evil.

Three years later, another popular book became a well-financed film with a new take on possession, and Brian DePalma brought his filmmaker's flair for stylish scenes and fine moments. In *Carrie* (U.S.A., 1976), demonic desires and psychic powers come to the aid of an unhappy young lady. Tormenting classmates and a repressive mother are dispatched in psychokinetic whirlwinds of fire and flying objects. Sissy Spacek is a natural actress whose ordinary face will become emblazoned with fury. Again, however, the possessed monster fails to live up to its looks for the onlooker. Despite the transformation and terrible assaults, we sense no dread from her appearance or direct participation as victims. We find ourselves rooting for the demon and merely wowed by what we get to watch. Story and its intended main experience are at odds with the horrific equation. Carrie is a likable protagonist, the original injured party, now empowered victim, and we are there for the vicarious thrill of righteous vengeance. Normally we become uncomfortable even when disliked characters are badly hurt, but not when we have bonded with the other side, a person still human and sympathetic. We not only painlessly enjoy the demise of unlikable people, but blithely accept the widespread destruction of innocent bystanders. The assaults are also softened by being run by remote control. Seeing Mother stabbed by a knife sent flying through the air is not the same as a savage thrust from Daughter's handheld blade. For the inborn image of alarm that grabs hold of our gut the weapon is part of the predator, and attack will be face-to-face with direct physical or surreal contact.

Despite so many demons, there are no undisputed champions in a field of mere contenders. The two box-office champs, highly promoted destroyers, tried to put on a good show, but pulled their punches. Formidable in appearance, they failed to knock their personal stamp on others. In what would become theatrical smack-downs, they simply slammed opponents with whatever was handy. They also picked on the wrong people. We don't see ourselves inside that ring. We are not those guys in turned-around collars who keep coming back to get clobbered when they could throw in the towel, and we certainly aren't those smug punks in high school who are so clearly asking for it. For all of their inexhaustible powers, these satanic beings fail to perform their most essential duties on us. We boo or applaud crowd-pleasing sideshows while sitting unscathed safely at ringside.

The desperate position of a bedeviled victim is far better realized in the forerunner of big-budget examples. Also based on a best seller, Roman Polanski's rendering of *Rosemary's Baby* (U.S.A., 1968) is strongly cast and crafted, and it creates sustained tension, mounting anxiety, and dreadful fright. A young newlywed discovers that the nosy old kooks across the hall are members of a satanic clan and that her career-minded husband has acquired his good fortune by selling her services as the devil's breeding ground. Highly unsettling circumstances close in on the pregnant woman, and they become our own. While beginning to create someone else, Rosemary is slowly losing herself—losing strength, understanding, control, and all her outside support. Selfhood is being stripped away, all but motherhood, the sole identity she will come to choose.

Although a compelling climax heightens her personal diminishment with all-encompassing surroundings, our fright continues to lack sensations of demonic forces. Rosemary's terrifying realization that her kindly old doctor is a member of the clan, being sure that we are seeing him standing by the phone booth while she calls for help, her dreaded return to the care of husband and old practitioner by a disbelieving new doctor, and the chilling view of her keepers silently slipping ahead of her during a last desperate dash for safety—these personally experienced events could be the product of any conspiracy. We are gripped by pressing predicaments without much feeling of their satanic origin. Witchcraft provides a good explanation, a strong story line, and, at most, an edge of eeriness to our experience. Other than a brief dreamlike scene of impregnation, we never see the devil as the agent of assault or any person or setting become a display of surreal forces, and our chilling reduction fails to assume an eerie occult form. The observation lacks criticism since here it is no failure. An intentional lack of supernatural sensations serves the story, keeping the character of our disorder true to the conflict. While including the devil, this fine tale is all about us, and no more dreadful anxiety is required to do us in.

Demonic beings have yet to evolve to their full potential. No outstanding creature has been born that attacks in the form of its own design. Not coincidentally, no definitive picture has been made that powerfully provides the fully rounded experience. Although some later films, such as *Poltergeist* (U.S.A., 1982), have had some success with satanic powers, we still lack a wholly satisfactory classic. The missing experience is best found within the midcentury bloom of low-budget pictures, little films where the demonic being is fully formed. Should we wish to play along, overlooking unlikelihoods and imperfections, we become encompassed in surreal sensations. *Devil Doll* (Great Britain, 1964) is a spirited little film that possesses the essentials. The Great Yorelli's puppet partner isn't any dummy, and it is about to take over the act. Little Hugo begins to assume life as well as command over the ventriloquist. Although its papier-mâché face is only slightly unpleasant at the start, the same stiff leer takes on demonic dimensions when the puppet is animated on its own. This walking, talking little devil becomes remarkably unnerving, and armed with a knife, the sight is horrific. What should be silly may be seen as real and terribly disturbing. Unlike the awful-looking little girl fighting exorcism, this is the whole menace undiminished by poor choice of victims and means of attack. Although lacking the consistency and qualities of classics, this and some other underfunded productions tower over the major motion pictures by force of their experience. Not only is the sensation more intense, but its nature is enormously more disturbing. We are within some ghastly, surreal nightmare of unbounded evil, one with the consumptive look and smell of satanic assault.

After escaping complete consumption by the devil, audiences were not so lucky with the deep blue sea. The modern era's second smash hit switched from an occult environment to a naturalistic setting, and the picture successfully projected an impression of personal participation. Set on a small island and in the surrounding sea, the film presents a primeval annihilator with a developing taste for summer's swollen population. *Jaws* (U.S.A., 1975) proved to be the horrific chiller's most powerful enactment of natural menace. Once again, an original classic assumed life by giving birth to a fresh embodiment of our twin terrors. Formidable in body and strength, sleek and swift, the great white shark is all dissolution and consumption. Its arrival instantly denies all of our defenses, and it aims to take part of us away or swallow our entirety. We need not even see the form fulfill its purpose to be struck by its design. Stripped and streamlined to primal essentials, its smooth shape extends to the dissolute face, erasing all features capable of showing any redeeming emotions. Confined to a still picture, the shark is less compelling than many other horrific superstars. Set in obsessive motion after its prey, however, it carries enough of the signals to make it, along with the similarly sculptured big snake, far more frightening than any other natural man-eater. Sent bursting through the surface, suddenly all chasm with dagger teeth, it wholly disarms any observer.

The making of the menace owes much to the producers, Richard D. Zanuck and David Brown. The creature took the biggest bite out of a healthy budget. Constructing and operating a mechanical monster was a multimillion-dollar commitment. No producer of fright films had ever even considered acceding to such extravagant demands by a performer. It would have been enormously more economical to employ a bit player, a small model or a real-life shark with no acting experience, but the miniature could not be animated with complete realism, and the animal would be difficult to direct, and both would have to be artificially integrated into the action by intercutting or superimposition. Even with the aid of a life-size head thrust at actors under attack, encounters would be incomplete and possibly unconvincing. The temperamental big star did drive up the budget, often refusing to follow directions and even taking an unexcused absence when it slipped away unnoticed out into deep waters. The high cost of casting an exact replica, however, was a wise investment. Remotely controlled by hydraulic umbilical cords, a matched set of imposing impostors could reproduce every feature, expression, and movement with absolute authenticity. Unconfined to the back lot of special effects or far reaches of the ocean, the shark was free to perform alongside the other players on location. The result was overwhelming. High finance and modern technology were put to far better use than in the occult productions. Demonic films demand less naturalism, and they spent themselves on repulsive realism and miscellaneous magic tricks. Here, however, available resources fundamentally strengthen the picture. This creature not only gained the proper appearance, but it was fixed to perform primal destruction of selfhood.

The producers also gambled on a young director. Steven Spielberg's first big-budget film is a bit uneven in its direction, turning to too much talk and trumped-up diversions between assaults. Some tension is lost, and an unsettling atmosphere is missing. Offshore, however, it unwaveringly holds its course, taking dead aim on our disturbance. Suspense becomes gripping and shock is delivered with more than technical finesse, and our diminishment is expanded by a variety of situations and shapes of encounter. The director puts us on the spot by centering on the position of the threatened person rather than the body of destruction. Little is seen of the shark in its opening rounds, but the sight of a swimmer suddenly yanked under with explosive force leaves us stranded in fear. Unlike the unladylike eviscerator waiting to strike at the Bates Motel, this one will make many appearances. Its full form is wisely withheld, allowing it to become increasingly overpowering with successive sightings. Saving the worst for later also enriches the experience with sensations that might otherwise have been missing. Remaining on the surface, being left with the emptiness of someone pulled under is a powerful envisioning of loss. This and other dimensions of our reduction would go unrealized if the director had joined his predator in a single-minded rush to completion.

The horrific being is always a collaborative creation. The high-priced model wisely approved by the producers and unusually well worked by the director sprang from a writer's conception. Peter Benchley's novel was nicely staged for the psyche, and particularly well set for cinema. Even its central setting is rich with visual triggers of alarm. Seashore and calm waters may be serene spots of rest and recreation with pleasant associations, but they also place us in a diminished position. Especially when swimming, but also on board, our standing is ripe for more reduction. Even on the lookout, we may be wholly unaware of what could be just a few feet away and, if alerted to danger, both fight and flight could be critically handicapped. Loss of immediate awareness and defensive capacity marks our posture with negative signatures. Any person seen in this position will greatly magnify the fright from a proximate threat. Danger does arrive, and it comes in the form of horrific experience. This setting is the home of a primitive predator designed to take full advantage of its domain. Reducing us on sight, shaped by dissolution and annihilation, it may undo its victims with the same imagery.

The story even shores up some deficiencies in this oceanic creature. Although bearing the desired blank look of voided humanity, one also ready to reveal a deadly abyss, the visage is less like us than the ultimate horror. It is also too naturalistic. The author is confined to a real-life presentation, but he prudently takes psychic license. This shark is larger than any previously seen great white, and, while remaining in range of possibilities, it assumes an unnatural aura of more than just animal. It may be no more than blind instinct, but the creature's relentless pursuit of those aimed at its destruction carries a chilling sense of human intelligence, obsession, and vengeance. Benchley's book enriched the equation of altered states in every part of the encounter. The configuration of the menace, the shape in which it will leave its victim, and even the form of the person's position beforehand visually trigger our primal alarm.

A few years later, a similar set of jaws would be encountered in deep space, and our spot was switched from being terribly wide open to one of inescapable confinement. With the passing of the fifties, UFOs were disappearing from the skies and screens. Soon in reality man would become the explorer, and any spaceships on-screen would be headed away from Earth. Improved budgets and special effects allowed actors to outdistance our astronauts with remarkable authenticity. A succession of space spectaculars reproduced all forms of adventure other than terror until *Alien* (U.S.A., 1979). The film stands as the most frightening picture set outside of Earth, a first-rate horror classic, and the title character is a growing, mutating creature with devouring jaws. One by one, the confined crew of a distant starship is consumed by the sudden appearance of a stowaway. Although the presentation is a bit thin and predictable, it is expertly crafted with surefire visualizations of primal consumption. Ridley Scott, an artist turned director of high-gloss commercials with powerful imagery, creates a picture short on substance with enormous visual and emotional impact. To his credit, the filmmaker overtakes the audience with little exploitation of grotesque details. A full view of destruction comes only in the creature's shocking entrance from inside its unwitting host. Breaking through the astronaut's belly, busting it wide with shocking realism, the alien is born. Before dashing out of sight with startling speed, it stands erect and confronts the horrified crew. We see a snakelike body and bulbous head with bulging, undeveloped eyes, and the snapping jaws of a piranha. The camera reveals little of the creature during its successful consumption of the crew. Quick glimpses establish that it continues to grow and metamorphose while remaining all teeth drenched in dripping fluid.

Our disturbance would have far greater range had the director been more concerned with changing the shape of our encounters rather than that of his predator. The intensity, however, is all there. Despite knowing what to expect and not having to see very much when it happens, viewers experience enormous discomfort as soon as a recognized setup lets them see it coming.

The notable upgrading of production values brought by big-budget extravaganzas soon included the lowliest examples. It was an industry-wide phenomenon. Double bills were gone, along with the category of B-pictures and low-budget look. Minimum financing was far less frequent within all genres, and a long overdue revolution in making production equipment portable, as well as advancements in film stock, significantly reduced the work while improving the result. There was no shortage of inexpensive shock films with a veneer of technical polish and lack of substance. Once again, the teenage audiences had swelled, and their tastes were of justifiable concern to every producer. Given the burgeoning costs of both making and marketing pictures, the industry grew fearful of financing any movie that might not include young people in its appeal, and there was profit in product aimed solely at this audience. Times had changed, however, since the last glut of inexpensive, youth-oriented horror films, and it brought more than improved production values. No longer were beach parties broken up by some bubble-headed creature. Now the teenagers paired off in bed and were hacked to death by someone nursing a grudge. High-schoolers, even when accompanied by a parent, still could not see any film revealing the whole human body, but children were invited to witness unclothed, sexually active young women being mutilated beyond recognition.

Hitchcock's knife-wielding maniac was confined to two victims, and what we saw was inspired cutting of imagery rather than slashing of bodies. A generation later, young people had learned to stomach brutal violence on-screen, and many developed an appetite, and there was no shortage of young filmmakers able to handle the task. Mindless mutilation replaced thoughtful construction of conflict, and it was usually the same picture. Serial murderers make repeated strikes, and that's about it. Some of these killers defy capture and even their own death, returning with the same old M.O. in a continuing series of pictures. For *Friday the 13th* (U.S.A., 1980–89) the fated date came up far too often. *Halloween* (U.S.A., 1978), however, was much more enjoyable, and the film is most often selected as the best low-budget shocker of the modern era. It certainly proved to be the most influential in popularizing hard-core catalogs of killings. The teen population of a small Midwestern town prefers to collect their Halloween goodies in bed, leaving it up to a lunatic to find a costume and scare people. The boogeyman wears a pale mask with the cut-out features of a crude jack-o'-lantern. A smooth surface voids any sense of humanity, while the angled eyes and frozen grimace announce animal predator. Body is oversized, with unusual strength and recuperative powers, and its single-minded obsession with annihilation cannot be missed. John Carpenter achieves a good look and nice film from meager funding, and devoting time to stalking and developing situations, he makes it considerably more frightening than most slaughter movies. The example, however, typifies its category by minimal concern with unfolding construction, striking viewers with a series of interchangeable assaults that lack a strong sense of deepening consumption.

The Next Generation

Despite an uninterrupted production of horrific films since *Alien,* a new century would arrive with no outstanding new classics possessing an original vision. Old creatures returned in less compelling pictures, and the new ones didn't do much better. No movie continued to grip everybody well after it was over with dark and deep dread. By the final decade stunning advances in technology allowed filmmakers to be limited only by their imagination, and that has proved to be the problem.

Although *Jurassic Park* (U.S.A., 1993) aimed more for adventure than horror, it was a big part of a new wave of fright films, and its strengths and what can be weaknesses typify the new environment for horrific creatures. Employing the wondrous talents of Industrial Light and Magic, Steven Spielberg once again advanced the art of fabricating fierce beasts and integrating them into expertly crafted sequences. Some full-scale models were employed, constructed with greater size and sophistication than the great white shark, but so were far more ethereal creations. Free-roaming dinosaurs and raptors on the run would have to await their arrival on film to assume final form. Frame-by-frame animation of small models proved to be too jerky for the highest standards of production. The positions of hundreds of points across their surfaces, however, were easily recorded, and, by connecting the dots into crosshatching lines, computers could generate the contours for painting the dinosaurs onto film. Software programs were improved and invented, and repeated passes through the computer would add external features and texture, the effect of skin and muscle passing across bone, jiggles and sway matching the momentum of movement, and, finally, the illusion that the animal was lit within the setting of live-action photography. The camera on location was tracked by computer. It could move into, around, and over the scene while a corresponding shift in perspective would match the yet-to-be-added livestock. A mobile camera usually enhances action, and here it also powerfully enforces the connection between real and concocted imagery in three-dimensional space. The two images fit together so precisely that dynamic interaction was simulated, ranging from the physical impact of being struck to the subtleties of eye-to-eye contact. This was by no means the first successful marriage of actual and virtual life-forms, but it was a dramatic breakthrough in reproducing real animals of such complex detail, movement, and expressiveness. The result was wholly authentic and truly amazing.

The ability to generate whatever one chooses enables the director to shape each shot precisely storyboarded for the most powerful presentation. Spielberg excels here as well, and his construction of suspense from simple elements, timing of surprise, and pacing of what unfolds are well designed for alarm. For such expertly crafted stalking and striking by awesome annihilators, however, the film's undeniable fright is surprisingly nonhorrific. The routine script need not have been more inspired to achieve horror had it written in darker elements and not provided an escape clause. No evil exists in the savage beasts or even in the men that brought them to life, and no aspect of the environment contributes to any aura of doom. Fashioned for a family audience, it soon reassures us with a sense that nice people will survive and that children not only will be spared, but may very well help save the day. Spielberg is a filmmaker with a personal vision and unusual abilities in all departments, but he is most at home with the glow of magical wonderment and spiritual connectedness than with our darkest sides. His heart is in the wrong place, instinctively siding with the sentiments of his audience and the lives of those we like on-screen over the unnatural appetites of what should be the horror director's favorite character. By design and default, a comforting context shields us from experiencing enveloping dread.

Generated imagery has created some scary designs, even good imagery for some not so good movies. Although a tongue-in-cheek adventure film, *The Mummy* (U.S.A., 1999) featured a genuinely horrific embodiment of decomposition and rebirth. The risen is all skeleton and clinging tissue with cavities exposing only emptiness inside. Emitting an awful roar, it can disconnect its jaws, ripping them apart into a gaping chasm with rotten teeth made unnaturally menacing. In *The Haunting* (U.S.A., 1999), an old estate, wonderfully grand and ornate with Victorian opulence and indulgence, provides a spooky setting that will reshape itself into a chilling display of danger and despair. So pure in compelling primal signatures, these and many other powerful creations could have been the core of memorable movies had they been given smart and dark screenplays. Well-conceived pictures, such as M. Night Shyamalan's chilling and thought-provoking *The Sixth Sense* (U.S.A., 1999), typically lacked a strong center of consumption.

Any next generation of classic fright films will arrive within this new age of film, one that shaped Spielberg's production. Computers can paint by the numbers every individual dot in a digital picture, and they made possible the rebirth of extinct reptiles and their seamless integration into staged photography. For better and for worse, spectacular effects are increasingly exploited. Their potential drawing power may justify their abundance, but too often amazing imagery undermines simple elements that worked well without help, and sometimes they seem to be the sole basis for productions showcasing stunts and pyrotechnics. Too often, product lacks its promised payoff. Given the amount of money on the line, one cannot help but be astonished by the number of inadequate screenplays approved for production in all genres, scripts that not only lack originality but even fail to put real people or places into the formula. Perhaps it is the money, the raised stakes in profits and losses that have handed too much of Hollywood over to experts who know business but not the show. Too many creative decisions are made by deal makers and money managers with insulated livelihoods and ancillary interests, and the result is updated data-designed hodgepodges of popular ingredients. Producers should not be blamed for seeking simple, surefire ideas that instantly sell themselves, but their failure to back all bets with attempts at superior storytelling is inexcusable. There is profit to be made from art in the formula and turning digital technology to this end. Once you can do anything, amazement will vanish from effects no longer special. Technology serving a dark story, however, finding new forms of the old design, will create an environment for more dreadful appearances.

Psychic Form and Function

It may pass for a person, but the signs of human absence and animalistic aggression will be seen. It may be another life-form or even normally nonliving matter, but humanlike features will be there. Born from a union between twin terrors, the creature adapted to changing climates and new environments, and every successful example tells its personal story with a new version of shared symbols. Form follows function in life's evolution, and when people's worst fright is the function, forms will be fashioned from three visual languages speaking to automatic emotion. Newborns will be all personal dissolution and primal extinction, and any menace missing these features will not survive. Prior to striking there will be no chilling sensations of irrational dread, and even primitive assault may be lacking in horror. Successful creatures must also reshape victims as advertised, by behavior and appearance remaining true to form, performing their only purpose by way of their design.

Selected films, arguably the best in their category, well express the genre's diversity. There are, of course, many other worthy choices, ones with terrible dread that becomes horrific. The reader may have personal favorites, and they could be better than some discussed here. Free to pick your best shot, sequence, or overall film, you will always select the same thing. It can be your present judgment of best picture or no more than a moment from childhood, a vision seen anywhere from the darkest movie to the mirror in **Snow White**. At the heart of the matter is that dissolute and driven being, all vital signs elevated, primed for your deflation.

XII. Close Relatives

Appearing in some chilling melodramas, there is a rare breed of unusually frightening people who call our findings into question. They are always sociopaths, but these ones stand out. In some uncanny way they are insidiously disturbing. They lack sinister features, and sometimes they are quite good-looking, but well before they hurt anyone, we will become terribly afraid. These smooth operators that look like us are not usually found in horrific chillers, but they are important to our understanding of the genre. Their riveting presence must either disprove the need for visual signatures or somehow stand as remarkable reembodiments of the rules.

Monster in Human Guise (a case study)

In more than a hundred appearances, Robert Mitchum played a good number of bad guys, but he also successfully portrayed nice leading men, romantic rogues of rugged and sensual appearance, stalwart military protagonists of the highest order, and older, hard-nosed investigators who, even if on the skids, full of self-doubt and cynicism, do not dispel our perception of integrity, compassion, and conviction. On two occasions, however, without benefit of menacing makeup or a horrific setting, he dominated the screen with a terrifying presence of primal proportions. For someone so often cast for positive physical features, this actor's ability to be seen as such an unsettling monster is an important challenge for what was thought proven.

In *Night of the Hunter* (U.S.A., 1955), Mitchum plays a drifter, con artist, traveling preacher, and false prophet. A boldly original film, it conforms to no conventional category, perhaps best described as a modern-day gothic fairy tale, a romantic celebration of pure and gentle goodness triumphing over the darkest forces of human nature. When Mitchum is in view, however, the picture is undeniably a terribly chilling fright film that leaves us badly shaken.

Harry Powell has a deal with his maker. He will spread a version of the Lord's word worked out between them, and the Almighty will provide him prey. This time it is a widow unaware of money hidden on her property and her two young children who know its whereabouts. With L•O•V•E tattooed on four knuckles of his right hand and H•A•T•E across the left, the preacher is all oppositions and single-mindedness. We will find him seated and scowling at a girlie show, the left hand slipping into his pants pocket and a switchblade slashing erect through the trousers. We will see him ingratiating himself with easily impressed townspeople, but his tone and demeanor are smugly contemptuous. We will hear him tell tall tales, but the theatrical edge to his delivery suggests a possible indifference to whether or not we believe him. Well-chosen words may even come from both sides of his mouth, such as sweet-talking the little girl about giving up the secret while sending clear signals of threat to the older brother. Always there is that velvet, bass baritone voice with deep resonance, a sound that is at once mellifluous and intimidating, and trivial sing-songy plati-tudes will be followed by low-pitched commandments to be taken most seriously. All of these contradictions come together in a high-tension body ready to spring, yet so unusually at ease with eyes half-asleep.

The preacher will marry the widow without any sign of affection, even humiliating her on their wedding night for expecting to consummate a holy union without the intent of begetting children. When she discovers his true intent, the very knowledge that would have saved her leaves her lost and defenseless. She is on her back in bed passively exposed in prayer when the switchblade is slowly driven to her neck. Before the pretender's eventual undoing by the pluck of a loving old lady and her adopted flock of children, the two orphans will be pursued relentlessly, in fear for their lives.

An artfully written and crafted picture strengthens Mitchum's deeply disturbing portrait. He finds far less support in *Cape Fear* (U.S.A., 1962), a more ordinary melodrama made memorable by the actor's painful presence. Here he is Max Cady, a man with contempt for all women and a long-festering loathing for the lawyer who failed to free him on a rape charge. Recently released from prison, Cady is ready to be repaid for his lost years and family. Laid back and brazen, he favors the slow application of pressure while you can only imagine what will come next, and he lets the lawyer know about the debt but not the cost. First suspecting extortion, the attorney soon fears for his safety before believing that it will be something worse for his wife or even teenage daughter. Intimidation and stalking will continue to tighten their hold, finally leaving the family separated and under siege at night in the swampy backwaters of Cape Fear.

Whether in earnest or at play, Cady's game is always the same. It is seen in a telling short scene unrelated to plot. In an idle moment over a cup of coffee he transforms the familiar banter found at any truck stop diner. He easily engages the friendly waitress in what we would hear as ordinary byplay were we not sensing something far from innocent, mindless, or normal. By well-scattered and individually harmless cues his moves are set in motion. Bemusement, innuendo, a glance at her body, the lowered voice and knowing grin—it is more than friendly. It is so craftfully intangible, yet in no uncertain terms, and he lets her know she is included in his private thoughts. Rambling on, he gives no concrete cause for complaint, but much to justify alarm. The poor woman need only to have caught the drift to show some of the discomfort that we have been feeling as mere observers. When she does, the signs are slight, but all that he needs. Any show that she understands where he is going is a confirmation of her dirty mind. She is down, and he strikes with a query about her wedding ring, followed by a slap of five dollars on the table and asking if she knows what it's for. Cady's triumphant leer knowingly acknowledges their shared understanding of what all women are. She is free to leave but cannot escape the laugh, deeply resonating self-satisfaction and derision. The waitress is released but the lawyer is not so lucky. The stalking is unrelenting, the innuendo worse, and Cady's amusement more serious. When the lawyer reluctantly resorts to hiring thugs to rough him up, Cady is left in better shape. The ex-con delights in seeing such an upstanding citizen reduced to lawless violence, a mistake that could strip him of his license and leave him unprotected by police. It is a reworking of what we saw with the waitress. Just out of reach, Cady is in our face with twisted suggestions that shake us loose from our foundations. Before we know it, we are down to his level, greeted with contempt for being there, and soon beaten at the game of his choosing and expertise.

The Perverse Predator

Although it is particularly disturbing that the preacher is so duplicitous, we can say the same for Cady being so boldly out front. What these two unusually unsettling individuals share proves to be more informative. In both people we see a sly stalker and a powerful predator with the attributes of a jungle cat. Exceedingly patient, alert while at rest, he is smooth and unruffled even under stress. He is crafty and calculating when stalking and is fearless and overpowering in attack. Even after the pounce, maneuvers may not be over. Quarry remaining still may be prodded to make them move. He likes to play, strike a nerve, pick away, and soften us up, then let us go or go for the kill. Nature's plan, of course, has been perverted. He preys upon his own species, and, unlike a predator's natural indifference to any pain it causes, this one seeks signs of our discomfort. It is a contempt fueled by a monstrously inflated ego, one that measures its standing against our loss. Whatever else he wants, he desires to disarm us. He delights in our diminishment and will always add insult to injury.

A callous narcissist and crafty sociopath out to hurt others describe all motives and behaviors, and there is a conspicuous lack of unrelated qualities. Limited dimensions serve these people. Every attribute propels their mission forward, and no other pastime or pleasure can send them sideways. Surely there is no trace of morality or sense of sympathy to give them pause. Even when taking their time or seeming to loiter, they are always gaining on their prey. The driving force of aggression is so well governed. Even strongly provoked, the impulse for anger will be denied should it interfere with a more calculated conclusion. When it comes, the violence is not blindly bestial, but controlled and ritualistic. Cady loses it for an instant with a call girl, his eyes exploding wide open as he silences her with a sudden flurry of slaps. Quickly collecting himself, eyelids dropping to their customary languid position, he is calm and thoughtful, rubbing his hands together while slowly circling the woman. His eyes are locked on hers, awaiting her acknowledgment that his unknown way has yet to come. The preacher also quietly circles his bride lying in prayer, his eyes following hers up toward heaven before the high-held dagger is driven downward in ritual sacrifice. From the moment that these assailants settle on their selection, continuing to a striking conclusion, it is all so smooth. While squirming in our seats, we cannot help but admire the outrageous audacity, self-serving righteousness, and silky finesse.

By any accounting there is much to fear from seeing this behavior, and by the primal formula it is everything. The perverse predator follows all the rules, more effectively, in fact, than some monsters in successful horror films. Most assuredly they make an assault upon selfhood. It is manipulation and oppression, engaging our complicity, preying on our weaknesses, and outmaneuvering our defenses. They hunger for our loss, looking to reduce us to nothing, not necessarily by physical harm, but by intimidation and contempt. Their success derives from stalking, extended periods of diminishment and dissolution, and an invasion of intimacy that strips us open. There is isolation, helplessness, and loss of normal control, and they know what will hurt us most. We assume the place of those easily reduced. The preacher preys upon blindly trusting females and defenseless children, while Cady chooses those ill equipped to deal with the darker forces in others or themselves. These agents of dissolution also specialize in our primitive and personal annihilation. Powerful and avaricious, if they leave you living, your sense of self will be scarred with their lasting signature. These aberrant creatures are humanlike beings with more than any ordinary obsession: an incorrigible, single-minded appetite for our incapacity and fright.

There is also the totalism, one where every trait serves the primal monster's defining identity. Even aspects that could set them apart are part of the same portrait. Their unusual skill and cunning is necessitated by such an exacting surgical operation on our selfhood. The rare conceit, fed by our inferiority, fuels the obsession and fires the desire for our dreadfully stretched out diminishment.

Even without any present threat, we are struck by the power of cocky self-confidence and cutting disdain, and such aggressively smug derision can put us down as firmly as a more energetic show of force. Well before something worse begins, reflexive reactions are automatically reducing our standing.

Although all of this is quite enough to be deeply disturbing, there has to be more. One way or another, we have seen it all before, often effectively executed by fine actors, but rarely is it so riveting. There must be a key ingredient not to be found in the script or every good performance, an aura beyond the measure of behavior, a forbidding presence always felt even without cause for alarm. There is something about the sight of him, and the dark and dreadful feeling is similar to confronting a fearsomely featured monster. The impression from seeing such sharp glances is part of it, but the thrust is deeper. The unsettling looks that on others would be no more than mere expressions appear here to be embedded in the body, formed by nature to be part of something alive with the same disturbing dimensions. Despite all that comes from a well-performed, scary screenplay, the menace is incomplete without its imagery.

Aura of Invincible Malevolence

Finding the shape of what we see begins with features inherent in the actor. Robert Mitchum was one of those uncommon performers who, with such economy of words and movement, is likely to command the screen and its sound track, and this powerful physical presence, one that is always so unusually at ease, forms the backbone of virtually every characterization. His broad-shouldered, tight-waisted, muscular body is tension and strength comfortably in control, relaxed and ready, without wasted motion even in a brawl. And it is the same with the face, ruggedly good-looking, yet oddly smooth, vacant and slow to commit itself. The drooping eyelids remain at rest, but there is evidence that he is always alert. It is a compelling sight, complemented by a voice of deep authority, rarely raised and always modulated by a velvet resonance. Even when seeming to sleepwalk through a throwaway performance, he may still hold our attention. His characterizations effortlessly exhibit what we felt we saw off-screen, a self-assured, no-nonsense kind of guy with little patience for pretentiousness or pussyfooting. It is a manner inseparable from the bearing, one creating a dynamic presence, sleepily electric, inner-directed, uncompromising, larger than life, and deadly serious. It is all projected so naturally and offhandedly that it is unquestionably real. When seeing these qualities in an aging, alcoholic private detective tackling his toughest case, we become completely confident of being in good hands. They are less comforting, however, when seen in a predator out to have a piece of us.

Whatever guise he takes, we find ourselves taken by a commanding force contained in an outwardly cool state. It is a power over us to reassure or to alarm, one always in control. The identical eyes are always there, surely significant by being so unusual, but depending on which one of his many characters has them, they will take on strikingly different meanings—the same windows into dissimilar souls. In them we see the relaxed and resolute military man on a mission or the over-the-hill, world-weary detective who will still rise to principle. Make him a heavy and, if he lacks intelligence, we see the empty eyes of brutish inhumanity. Introduce artifice and guile, and we suddenly see it, now finding coldly calculating concealment behind those lowered lids. Suggest indulgence or perversion and it is instantly spotted in the dissolute droop of a dissipated sensualist. Give him the inflated ego and that is there as well, with the unmistakably removed and above-it-all attitude of a true psychopath. Confirming and deepening how we view their different owners, the eyes have it, and being so at ease, they will always express that unconcerned confidence in having what it takes.

The troubling gaze appears in a face that is often made more disconcerting by asymmetrical expressions. The rest of him is also flexible, with two ways to go when aiming to overcome others. The primitive face is so smooth, the rugged body so graceful, it is surely someone who can get the job done in the trenches or where only cunning is called for. Both abilities will come together, along with that cool, commanding presence, in his two terrifying appearances.

Garbed all in black with a wide-brimmed cleric's hat, seen silhouetted on a distant rise mounted on a stolen horse, the preacher is a forbidding sight. Viewed closer, the starkness persists in the stern face, slit eyes, and tight lips, a countenance soon to be seen as decidedly callous and cruel. Attired in a sporty short-sleeved shirt and Panama hat, Max Cady's look is less severe, but the frame is the same, and the visage still displays those lowered lids and a signature expression. On Cady, the preacher's scowl is turned up in a smirk while similarly twisted in contempt. Even empty of expression, a blank stare from that stony face is disconcerting, and it does not take much, an inappropriate grin or an arched eyebrow, to be most troubling. Even the poker face is far from vague, and Mitchum's correct choice of the wrong reaction is a dead-on display of an aberrant nature. Subtlety and slowness of expressive changes on this partially blank slate leave much up to us. Once we know where he stands, however, without words and sometimes in spite of them, the face tells all, and so does the body. Seen mostly submerged, slipping through reeds at night, silently swimming across swampy waters of Cape Fear, bare-chested with muscles smooth and oily, exhibiting ease and economy of movement, he has a look that cannot be denied. It ripples through his body and every aspect of his behavior, the lithe predatory cat cunningly and relentlessly pursuing the hunt, whose cold kill is almost anticlimactic. The still face of the stalker lit by marbled moonlight is the smoothly sculptured contours and ominously empty gaze of a panther. The only times in either picture that the eyes will open wide are the rare occasions that, near to his prize, he is jolted by an unforeseen gain or an unexpected denial. The sound is animalistic. There is that deep velvet purr heard in his voice of contentment, the yelping barks when hit by buckshot, and the growl when held at bay. Mired in a muddy thicket while the two orphans slip away downstream with the money, the preacher is left stricken, his humming moan becoming more human, a wail rising in pitch before exploding into a horrifying scream of absolute loss.

Nearly thirty years after its original release, *Cape Fear* (U.S.A., 1991) returned to the screen with a top-notch cast in the hands of a master director, Martin Scorsese. Robert De Niro honed his formidable talents on intimidating roles, and his Cady has an appropriately seedy and unseemly air about him. He also methodically enacts the same assaults on selfhood within a far more powerful overall presentation. On his own, however, De Niro is much less disturbing than Mitchum. The original ex-con stands out in a crowd, and even at ease in a nonthreatening situation, he will come to resonate unsettling imagery. As always, Mitchum arrives with that cool and commanding presence and a face easily suggestive of other qualities. We need only know his motives and see him relate to people for the predator to be completely visible. It is all out there in a brutish face that has the inherent shape of detachment, dissolution, and deception. Add a few expressions, and we see that unbounded ego all too ready to render us helpless. In addition to his often underrated acting abilities, Mitchum appears so comfortably at home in uncompromising roles because his solid and relaxed embodiment is cast so perfectly true to form. When bent by distorted nature and harmful purpose, the actor's given air of unusual authority becomes an aura of invincible malevolence. Whatever that body has in mind, there is no getting around it. Its irresistible impulse is unavoidable.

Embodiments of Contextual Completion

The horrific being is identified by an unnatural aura of alarm that rivets our attention. For humans it takes various forms. Typically and most powerfully, aberrant features are displayed. They are usually there all the time but may be introduced by physical transformations or even by our point of view, such as seeing the slasher's face voided by a curtain. A related, far less intense feeling may be attached to an individual who remains ordinary in appearance. Any agent of shocking experience will become a disturbing presence by continuing to carry some of our earlier emotions with them. Far more insidious than this invisible air, approaching the force of graphically unnatural monsters, are embodiments waiting to be completed in our mind's eye by no more than information. Some people who might even appear to be attractive, when seen in the context of what we come to know about them, will be found to have primal signatures of dissolution and aggression. It is the same as encompassing possibilities in a scene. Something says danger, and alerted senses find alarm in what had seemed to be safe. Formerly benign features assume a life of their own, their psychic form shaping our reduction.

Features and mannerisms will come to exemplify what we see inside any person, and by their association come to send the same feelings, even become proof of our main impressions. It happens with loved ones, and it can go opposite ways with controversial public figures, even presidents. Whatever side you're on, the more you see of them, their faces and bearings come to exhibit your views so clearly, become so obvious, that you can't imagine why the other side can't see it.

We know what we see, and signs identified in context are seen to be as good as any others. In the context of alarm, required evidence is reduced. Symbolic signs assume enormous significance, and what was meaningless could become the sight of something serious. When perverse predators assault the most intimate aspects of selfhood, their primal behavior enormously empowers any compatible psychic features. Especially on the face, the signs need not be strong, easily disregarded on anyone else, but here their meaning cannot be overlooked, and it tellingly flies in the face of any pretense of another persona. Despite their making so much method out of madness, psychopaths still need to give a good show of visual signatures. Although it's not always detected on first sighting, the standouts will always have it.

People who will come to disturb us most enter as individuals whose given form and demeanor calls us to attention with their unusually commanding, though not necessarily intimidating, presence. When these disarming figures come to be seen with the psychic signs of negation, the physical foundation is so powerful and real that all features fashioned from it assume enormous force and credibility. The embodiment need not take the shape of Mitchum's vacant face and raw power under such relaxed and tight control. It will usually be tall, but can be slender, possibly with deep-set eyes and a hushed voice and strident scream. If small, it may have piercing eyes and will be more energetic or agitated, swift, sure and voracious, darting out unexpectedly in a frenzied assault. Whatever form it takes, in the person we will see a predator properly put together for its perverted purpose.

The stalker must be free to roam polite society. Camouflage goes with the territory. For success with people watching the movie, however, there must be enough gaps in the sheep's clothing to expose the true colors of predator. Once the field marks have been spotted, they will set him apart from the merely murderous. Now simply knowing his intent makes us shrink from his presence, and when he stalks or strikes there is an added dimension of horror. The character and power of emotion turns out to be entirely consistent with the formula. We are confronting a humanlike creature that embodies as well as enacts selfhood's dissolution and primal extinction. For the horrific being it is always a matter of appearance, but some will fit who, seen in another setting, may have the look of an admirable individual. In a disturbing context we will see it. There is the dominance of noted universals, the same primal signatures of emptiness and assault, and those dreadfully unsettling sensations. There is that totalism in which every evident physical feature contributes to a primal form that mirrors its behavior. This fixed visual identity inherent in the being is unmistakable in both of Mitchum's appearances, and in one even his outfit is cut from the same cloth. The clad-in-black preacher, stark specter of darkest designs, this cold, unflinching statue, primitive and powerful with smoothly polished surface and stony face—years later, long after pieces of plot have left us, there still is no escaping the sight and sound of him.

XIII. The Making of Emotion

Arts and crafts count even in generic creations, and there are qualities that distinguish the best examples. Chillers entwine us in a tapestry of terrifying designs, and the bonds of their spellbinding fabric may be strengthened by the selection of threads and the way they are woven. Embroidering in some optional lines may be helpful, but the greatest hold is tied to what we will always see. Skill in fashioning just a few parts of a common picture significantly adds to the entirety, and to our entanglement and emotions.

Organic Construction and Timing

When movies began telling stories, they were pure imagery and all timing. This essence of film is the heart of the chiller, a genre in which pacing and flow of images is critical. Horrific films that succeed follow the same course in a similar journey, and any sequence that provides the entire experience is also an ordered succession of the same stages.

Good examples of scenes are plentiful, with *Psycho* offering some of the most viewed and best remembered. Following a woman's disappearance, someone we have seen stabbed and disposed of, a detective has entered the picture and is now on his way into the deranged killer's home. It is also our first look inside, and our tension is terribly elevated by the intruder's complacency. After a quick perusal downstairs, the man ascends the steps, heading toward where he has seen old Mother Bates at the window. He is near the top when, without warning, a frenzy is upon him. The shriek of music, knife to the head, we are propelled from our seats and then denied quick recovery by a prolonged, almost surreal shot where we float down the staircase with the bloodied-face victim. Tripping backward, but still oddly erect, the detective does not collapse until reaching the landing, and then, once again, the annihilator is all over him. In a final brief close-up of raised arm and butcher knife, the blade is repeatedly driven downward out of frame.

The sequence contains all the ingredients of serial construction: context, premise, tease, build, revelation, extended climax, and cap. Here the context is the setting, a place associated with shocking violence. Lacking context there would be little suspense, no sense of the man's intolerable lack of concern, and unforeseen assault might leave us more stunned than deeply disturbed. A premise is employed to heighten jeopardy, and here it is innocence of surroundings. Scenes usually add a tease. If the character is aware of danger, it may be a false alarm, or, if nobody knows what is waiting, we alone may get a peek. In this scene, however, terrifying imagery from the shower is still with us. We would welcome hints that would soften any shock, and the very absence of discovery becomes a tease. The build works the founding elements, prolonging the period with drawn-out and mounting tension. Here the build is the detective's slow climb that seems so interminable, one making us wish to call out a warning. At the peak of our elevated anxiety, we are still caught completely off guard by a sudden revelation. True to the best revelations, it surprisingly confirms what was given, realizing our fears while exceeding all expectations. We have a new character who by strict convention will come to crack the case, and we are unprepared to see him so quickly relieved of his duties, an event almost as unseemly as the one earlier, when the main movie star and seemingly central character was so rudely unseamed and cut from the picture. The moment is maintained in an extended climax from which we are no more able to escape than the victim, swept downward in a strange and compelling shot that is more than mere documentation. Finally, it is all quickly capped by the maniac's renewed attack. Caps need not be more shocking, merely brief and decisive, an exclamation point punctuating the conclusion with a stroke of dramatic finality.

Construction may be as crucial as subject matter. Depending upon their arrangement, horrific events can be depicted without deep alarm, and more ordinary occurrences may become circumstances of high anxiety. An orderly development of disorder must occur. Missed steps may short-circuit our response, and each one must be properly played out and paced. There is no other form of filmmaking where precisely timed unfolding is so important, save sequences of physical comedy. Most wonderfully realized in the silent era and early days of sound, their sight gags and slapstick still destroy an audience with the ferocity of a shocker. Picturing calamity, funny or frightening, all comes down to timing, and the comedic film dismantles us with the developmental formula of its evil twin. In visual comedies, we also see a world a bit warped, bent in one direction, but still behaving by the rules. Here a context tells us that no one will be badly hurt, that the insults will be bruised egos and backsides rather than frontal assaults on their entirety. The nature of the person in trouble will be automatically part of a premise. The individual is likely to be a puffed-up superior due for deflation or someone as ordinary as ourselves pressing stoically forward out of sync with surroundings. A tease sets the stage for disruption and for us to start imagining outcomes. A build, often by adding elements to thicken the plot, milks the gag and heightens its tension while delaying the inevitable. Suddenly everything unexpectedly collides in complete calamity. Not entirely what was expected, but an even better resolution of all that was set up, the revelation provides an explosive release of pent-up emotions compounded by the surprise. Before we regain composure, the classic sequence may be extended by a chain reaction of unavoidable events and then capped, perhaps by a topper.

It is the same for comedic storytelling without pictures, well-crafted constructions of setups, teasers, punch lines, and toppers, or for any extended wordplay that disrupts the calm of conventional correctness with smart observation or some unmitigated silliness. Building amusement or alarm that gets to our gut has been orchestrated with the same rhythm and arrangement, all with an insidious timing fine-tuned to our reactions. Good humor has bad intentions. Even when probing painless areas, surgical inspection cuts clean to the bone, and then holds what's exposed up to ridicule. At the movies, we may sense the similarities between comedy and fright when finding a prolonged sight gag unusually suspenseful or feeling a horrific scene take on qualities of black humor. Our experience is all quite visceral, an involuntary response of organic emotion, triggered, shaped, and stretched with nuances and inflection. Impelled by suggestion, pulled by anticipation, gathering in momentum pressing for release, sometimes turned over and around, taking twists and turns while inexorably heading headlong only one way, it continues to create more bits and pieces that will take explosive shape in an instant shock of recognition. The revelation may be extended one beat or more, only to be capped or topped with quick closure, and a silence that leaves us resonating with it all.

Jack Benny observed that his job was made easy by an audience that always began chuckling the moment he walked on stage. Master of the long pause, short response, and prolonged reaction, that delightful put-on of a put-upon persona, the sight of his signature entrance with that sissy walk would stir our insides with surges of past emotion. It is no different with people who have overtaken us by terror or with settings and situations now reshaped by frightening experience, although comedy may ask more of the actor and place more restrictions on the filmmaker. Benny benefited from a pose, poise, and unsurpassed timing that was self-assumed, not put together from pieces of film. Laughter arises in part out of an appreciation for the performer. This was well understood by the great practitioners of physical comedy who insisted on playing it out on one shot, showing it all really happening, demonstrating that such untidy disorder is by the pure grace of an artist, a juggler, dancer, and high-wire performer completely in command of a calamitous ballet. Too often today we see foiled attempts to create similar gags in the editing room, employing comedians who lack the needed character and finesse to make it on their own. A frightful performance, however, is not supported by any awareness of the man behind it. Show business, talent, and trickery should be farthest from our thoughts when completely taken in. The scene may be sliced into tiny pieces, the best perspectives cemented together, and everything ordered and timed for the most powerful presentation. When the pacing of pictures is the main product, the contributions of editor and cinematographer are best realized. And the director may take it in the best direction, shaping key scenes and the whole film by the same steps of unfolding construction.

Perhaps the best way to create compelling scenes of our demise is to stop trying to write action and start composing music of dark emotion. Name that tune you want to hear—its distinctive tone and melodic flow. Choose the central chords that must be struck, ones with all the right reverberations, and then score it all in pictures. First envision an environment with many angles on it, views expressing the various moods you are after. Different parts of the place should give different impressions, visually frame people in different primal designs, and some parts should physically heighten actual peril. Find a coherent line of action well fitted to these particular spots, and to the notes you wish to play. Tune action and imagery together. With matching emotion, have changing events shown in shifting snapshots of the setting—a succession of real and symbolic portraits of personal disappearance—and make every key rhythmic beat a powerful reframing of assault. The best locations also provide differing viewpoints of danger. Far more powerful than the camera choosing to reveal bits and pieces is to see our annihilator change while on the way. Select places with different lighting, shadows, veils, or reflection to create distinct pictures of the menace's design. Employ the terrifying transformations of its appearance in tune with developing views of the victim's diminishment. Finally, feel the rhythm in the arrangement; see how each image sounds and how long it should remain in play. Correctly composed, the sequence will be a particular form of decomposition—a complete piece orchestrated with the tone and tempo of some dreaded departure.

Visualization of Key Perspectives

The first moving pictures, seen as so amazingly real, could never be confused with actuality. In addition to the absence of color, these were grainy renderings of soft resolution, imagery sometimes washed out and pale, other times heavy in contrast, and always lacking detail in abnormally bright and dark regions. This texture worked wonderfully with any unnatural subject matter of silent chillers. In a world where shapes are less sharply defined, where even emptiness shudders with granular mass, ghostly forms appear at home, naturally arising out of the ether of their environment. Living evil embodiments assume similar dimensions, and, in high-contrast relief, odious dark features dig into and etch out ashen faces in a most disturbing manner. The settings also benefit. Towering domains of long shadows, desolation, and decay are made more mysteriously impressionistic by diffuse areas of misty grays and murky blacks. All of this, however, would soon change. The development of high-resolution lenses and fine-grained black-and-white film with wide tonal latitude brought everything sharply into sight. Be it the frail, fine fabric of cobwebs against an ancient castle's cold interior of rough stone, the gleaming glass and luminescent electrodes in a more modern laboratory, or the bleak, muddy landscape of a moon-lit moor, the emulsion captured the feeling of every element.

Although the dreamlike quality was lost, the remarkable new richness and detail was well exploited. Movies were now staged and crafted within a studio setting, and the Hollywood look exhibited sumptuous art direction with the lighting and sensuously distinctive surfaces reminiscent of Rembrandt paintings. With a few modifications, the pictures became more evocative of Goya's dark sketches. Usually employing strong side light with elongated shadows, they were often boldly underlit, with areas of total darkness. Fearsome figures might be backlit silhouettes or have facial features reshaped by shadow. Wide-angle lenses with broadened perspective stretched out the space, while their deep focus extended from close-up to the most distant background. Lowered and elevated camera positions created disconcerting viewpoints that could magnify the menace and diminish threatened people. Impenetrable spaces became key to composition, while what we could see was ominously molded by dark casting of illumination.

In its midcentury revival, due to lowly budgets and the turn to modern settings, the genre lost its lavish look. There were the rare exceptions: Roger Corman nicely kept the look alive and decaying in *The Masque of the Red Death* (Great Britain, 1964) and other worthy examples. Few productions could afford cinematographers, designers, or directors with lengthy track records of notable achievement, let alone anyone comparable to the pioneering artists who had shaped the style. The rules of lighting and composition, however, had been set, and many were easily followed even by black-and-white B-picture exploitation films. The power of these patterns proved themselves again. Uninspired formula photography still served the picture, drawing us in and intensifying experience. And when rising above routine visualization, silly conceptions could become quite alarming.

Eventually high production values would be reintroduced in a modern bloom of big-budget productions, and, once again, fright films would be fashioned by those with the time and talent to craft every element. Examples now came in color, and along with the absence of artificial effects, the picture was crisp, rich, and real-life. Since reminders that it's only a movie can break the spell, it is widely assumed that every step toward realism is a move in the right direction. The assumption is false, and sometimes the reverse is true.

Imagine seeing a film set inside a spaceship, a picture with the virtually real reproduction that we have come to expect. A few crew members have barricaded themselves from those who have risen from the dead with a taste for their living comrades. The fully illuminated, flatly lit chamber is rendered with true color and clarity that bathes us in the glow of its shiny surfaces. Compare this look with the crude presentation of a similar situation in *Night of the Living Dead*'s farmhouse. Here we see colorless imagery, amateurish camera work and lighting, the rough grain of 16mm photography, and a high-contrast muddiness exaggerated by reprints and blowup. The imagery is enormously less realistic and professionally polished, yet it excels in the making of emotion. The whole scene of assault is far more frightening. What we see within the spaceship is remarkably like being there, but the evenly lit, antiseptic interior provides no ominous tonality, and the accuracy of reproduction fails to add any surreal suggestions. The muddy impressions inside the farmhouse prove true enough to take us entirely, and its rough, graphic rendering heightens the sinister nighttime setting while bringing a disturbing texture that removes us from any ordinary experience. Even the zombies are more dreadfully real due to their very lack of clarity and naturalism. Much would be lost by cleaning it all up and adding color and crispness.

The most effective visualizations share many qualities more important than realism. The first is a distinctive appearance, even if not inherently disturbing. Chillers take us to a place with unnatural designs upon innocents, a place, ideally, that is not the same as any other. Not all stories are able to provide central settings with unsettling shapes and shadowy illumination, but even those without any obviously ominous atmosphere will profit from an individualized look. Unusual signatures in the surroundings or photographic style separate us from the commonplace, and the imagery that sets this spot apart becomes a part of what it holds. When linked to terrifying events, every unique aspect of their look will come to echo their experience and independently add to emotion.

The distinctive imagery should not, of course, work against what is wanted with nice associations and peaceful qualities. The nostalgic feel of old photography is one example. Sometimes achieved by shooting the scene through a silk stocking, it brings softened colors, contrast, and sharpness warmed up with a sepia tone. Unwisely employed in *Burnt Offerings* (U.S.A., 1976), this prettified picture associated with romanticized sentimentality, coming with pleasant, pale impressions and a comforting lack of deep shadows, significantly diminishes the offering. A wide variety of looks, however, will work, even when they are initially neutral. Something unusual in the scenic design or way it was photographed makes this place unique, becomes part of the impression of being there, and remains as a constant reminder of the spot that we are in. And even at a later date, during the film's revival by recollection, the distinctive setting or style of imagery is still part of the experience.

The strongest individual shots frame a person's diminishment with a dangerous design. By the dynamics of composition and other evocative elements, they connect conflicting forces and graphically convey the attitude and power of all sides of the confrontation. What we find to be eye-catching compositions for any pictorial, pleasing or threatening, abstract or representational, provide a powerful pattern for the whole horrific scene. Compelling visual arrangements often triangulate three points of attention, and in chillers these may be a reduced person, an inflated evil embodiment, and a central component of the environment. This dynamic design, as well as others, highlights essential elements and well expresses the conflict's primal nature. In a space made less secure by its openness or enclosure, threatening and threatened forms are joined. Especially when rendered with dramatic angles and perspectives, their different postures, positions, and sizes in the frame will be compared, and the result is a measure of their disparate powers and dispositions.

The whole impression of this picture is always more forceful when the entire frame is fleshed out into a whole field of conflict. With its edgy sense of claustrophobic boundaries, the screen's original squarer shape is ideal for our desired frame of mind. Perfect for powerful triangular compositions, it tightly confines close confrontations while providing needed room above—a raised ceiling whose oppressive weight may be felt in close-ups as well as in long shots that isolate the figure in expansiveness. The wider the picture, the greater the challenge to maintain much needed height without unemployed side spaces diluting the totality. Even in a still picture of well-separated shapes, however, the sensation of interconnectedness will strengthen while we watch. We may connect combatants by following their lines of attention, attitude, or movement. It will also work without these cues, closing connections made by us, reinforced and cemented as our eyes dart reflexively from one key point to another.

The best pictorials present more than generic outlines of a diminished figure locked in the embrace of a looming embodiment and enveloping environment. By some highly evocative element, or by the whole fabric of the illustration, the entire picture is shaped to more specific forms of dread. Sometimes opposition will be here, conflict within imagery or ideas. When a spacious, fully carpeted boudoir and bath, all white and antiseptic, becomes the scene of bloody murder, the sight of crimson splatter stands out in startling visual contrast, and the idea of safe sanctuaries is shockingly contradicted. More often the frame contains compatible features. The psychic shape of some given danger is enhanced. Whether it is a sense of separation, containment, engulfment, invasion, absorption, consumption, diminishment, fracture, evisceration, decomposition, evaporation, or other eerie feelings of undoing, surrounding images may show the shape of danger, where we are now, or what we will become. Whether by art direction, lighting, or texture of reproduction, these impressions may arrive from any part of the picture.

While suffering psychic suggestions directed at the victim, the viewer may also experience actual diminishment. Observers will be put to a direct disadvantage by sights that are disorienting or beyond complete understanding, or keep some of themselves hidden by framing, obstruction, or shadow. And the illusion of imagery becoming our space will be seen when we find ourselves attempting to peer around something or shift our perspective.

In addition to incompleteness, everything can come together in a single shot. With a unique signature look, compositions commanding our attention regardless of content, conforming depicted danger to an inborn model of alarm, enhancing the apparent power of the enemy and weakness of its victim within an enclosing or exposing space, also charges the whole uncomfortable arrangement with specific sensations of its awful aim on us.

One way or another we will witness the stripping of selfhood, and as soon as it unfolds with primal imagery, we and what we see will be transformed. If our arrival at an old, dark farmhouse followed another night with its elderly inhabitant, a man with a liking for long knives and faces peeled off his victims, we are ready for surreal assault. What would have been no more than an unsettling atmosphere is now the unnatural essence of nightmare. Long, overhanging tree limbs appear to be bent for downward attack. Spindly, naked branches casting jagged shadows across the dilapidated dwelling may be seen as the grasp of awesome-size hands with sharp, elongated fingers set to slash. The rusting remains of a hay baler looming in the foreground strike with similar impressions. Rising out of tall grass in an abandoned wheat field, long and slender blades curl toward us in great arcs of identical alignment. Surely shaped to grab and cut, it is also suggestive of life long gone, an enormous ribcage now encrusted with its own erosion. This sense of seeing both annihilator and its aftermath is impossible to avoid in the scarecrow. Lifeless, still standing, its flat, cut-and-sewn patchwork face unshaped by any inner skull, this is a vision of victim. It is also the collector of our faces, still and silent, guarding its domain while waiting to strike, its face faithfully revealing inner aberrations and absence of humanity. Not far away, the farmhouse door repeatedly welcomes us with warnings by opening partway and blowing back shut. If we accept the invitation to enter, it will be a passage through decay into deep shadows, an emptiness hiding what might hurt us while displaying the very state of our coming disappearance. We become increasingly enveloped by more of the same, an atmosphere animated with dreadful intent while frozen in its outcomes, the beginning and the end.

While watching what should be a credible drama, we may become absorbed in the simultaneous presentation of a less likely scene. Action occurs within our innermost world of irrational realities and symbolic transformations, where anything may be more than one thing at once. It is a place where, even at a distance, agents of annihilation are invested with unnatural powers, and their lifeless surroundings will become enlivened with disturbing portent and purpose. It is where we once were, when all identities, including our own, were shapes of sensory experience, and our personal boundaries were easily invaded from anywhere. Any strong display of psychic signatures instantly introduces this deeper picture, and the scene beneath the surface infuses its emotion into the cover story. Times of relative safety are infected with eerie uneasiness, and any signal of possible attack may be wrought with dreadful diminishment.

Although unnaturalism in imagery is more easily accepted in science fiction or supernatural dramas, it may be introduced into realistic circumstances. Visualizations may alter normality in ways that do not stand out from the part of the picture reviewed by reasoned perception, yet cannot be missed in the primal presentation. Photographic lenses with focal lengths unlike our eyes are useful. They may warp space with unsettling results, enhance the enemy, and alter our boundaries. The wide-angle lens's deep focus and exaggerated perspective stretches out from where we stand into a pulled-apart landscape. Unnatural both in its expansive scope and deepening distance, it isolates us at the apex of its envelopment. Should we sense any safety in distance so dilated, this illusion will be shattered by another one. Anything coming right at us, even at a steady rate of speed, suddenly seems to close the gap with a quickening rush of acceleration and swelling in size. Equally disconcerting viewpoints may be formed by the telescopic lens. Here a narrowed field of view enlarges and flattens what we see in a compressed perspective. Distant danger appears to be awesomely inflated, and advancement in our direction is so strangely slowed that it may be seen as a display of relentless pursuit, even obsessive intent within nonliving objects.

Some stories may allow for the inclusion of video documentation, best done here with imperfect reproduction. Poor recordings can create agitations by their evocative additions along with frustrating refusals to reveal telling parts of their picture. They might be all black-and-white dots with little detail or the stark etching of luminous colors, sharp with trailing blurs of motion, sometimes with bright whiteouts and always those murky blacks. They may suddenly introduce incompleteness or electronic disorder within the scene, then all aflutter before flopping back into shape. And whatever alterations are added come with the vivid sense of immediate reality carried by television.

Although only acceptable in short dosages, extreme aberrations may be justified by natural causes. Warped visions can express the point of view of a disoriented victim. Viewing an assailant through a misty curtain or rain-drenched window, or seeing him reflected from a cracked mirror or bent surface, may create an impression of unnaturalism that persists throughout the film.

A sense of surrealism may also arise simply by the power of distilled imagery. When the whole picture approaches abstraction refined down to its insidious elements, we are overtaken by more nightmarish sensations. A bold composition of simple graphics provides a compelling exhibition of primal signatures, and its indelible impression is undiluted by any irrelevancies that might catch the eye. The absence of distraction strikes us twice. Fixing our attention on images of automatic emotion, it strengthens the grasp of their irrational invasion. Worse still, it creates an unadorned universe of elemental attributes, all shapes of sensation unnaturally focused and empowered that amplify everything with dreadful desire. We are enveloped by absoluteness.

Simple scenic design with sparse features is often best. When multifaceted details are important, such as the tiniest components of a spaceship, treating them more as surface texture of larger forms will help to shape an uncluttered frame. Black-and-white photography strengthens the abstraction and other key perceptions. Fundamental forms and forces become far more commanding when we cannot focus on color, and this unvarnished world of stark shapes, gray life, and dark places is full of frightful meanings. Filters on the lens can create unnatural contrasts taken to be real, such as casting brilliant, white clouds against an unusually dark sky. Accepted as a truthful rendering while allowing normality to be altered, monochromatic imagery is insidiously subversive, quietly assisting our unquestioning descent into the surreal. Unfortunately, for far too long, black-and-white has rarely been employed for theatrical films. Directors continue to appreciate that films of fright could profit, but the fear among producers is that revenues would not.

It is widely agreed that the best cinematography does not call attention to itself, serving instead the story and the director's take on it. Although this applies to all narrative pictures, the chiller's story is its imagery. Primal designs viewed by primitive perceptions and understandings tell their tales to our deepest emotions and involvement. Visualization remodels what will be our universe for the next two hours, refashions its forces, and may even reshape the form of injury that we feel. The selection of style is usually suggested by subject matter, but even when they demand everyday realism, chillers also call for an unnatural rendering. This is not necessarily a conflict. Film noir wonderfully combined the two in a look that is also applicable to terror. Created for the more savvy and tough-minded audiences of the postwar forties, the genre took aim on the corrupt underbelly of society where people on both sides of the law and all stations acted out dark forces residing within all of us. The visual style was strong graphics by the power of light and darkness. Simple source light from the side, back, or overhead sculptured and silhouetted what was seen. Slashes of light and dark sliced up the screen with clean lines at sharp angles, balancing bright areas with shadow spaces. This was a stark, black-and-white sketch, the stripped-down naked truth, moody and uncompromising in tonality. With light seemingly limited to sources within the scene, not softened by any artificial fill, a feeling of documentary realism and hard-edged honesty illuminated its sense of true-life subject matter. This neorealism, however, was bold abstraction, pure and simple, keeping it real while empowering the irrational.

Not all chillers should be taken so far. Some even require a cunning subtlety, but well below the threshold of obvious artifice or artiness there will always be room for a stylized reality. In this age of explosive commotion and overfed sound tracks, it is easy to get by and even impress, and it is tempting to take the technological course of increasingly accurate reproduction. It can be done better. Cinematographers would do well to measure what they fashion against four qualities found in all of the best examples. The strongest visualizations establish an individualized look that, even if not suggestive of disturbance, supplies its own signature. They employ confrontational compositions that magnify the differences between the sides and make space less secure. They will also exhibit graphic symbols and disturbing textures that send the unique sensations of a specific form of reduction. Finally, they approach abstraction without distraction, stripped to its essentials. Revealing a simplicity deeper than the smallest details, they exceed the sharpness and accuracy of any ordinary photography. By additions and subtractions, these enhanced reproductions more clearly reveal the true realities.

Although only primal signatures trigger our deepest disturbance, good imagery may convey many other agitations. A striking shot may contain unreconciled tensions not connected to our model of alarm. Conceptual conflicts, the suggestion of ideas not normally seen together, may create some unsettlement as we try to combine two viewpoints in our heads. Emotional discordance is sure to jar us when differing, highly evocative elements trigger feelings not normally felt at the same time. Unrelated to content is how the scene is framed. Even for pure abstractions, the brain is most comfortable when the center of attention is well centered, and edgy compositions create their own unease. Artists with cameras will find places to embed the primal picture with contradictions and disruptions, the pulse of unnatural arrangements, an added punch of personal chemistry to the powerful generic.

Hooks, Lines, and Red Herrings

Our deliverance to being served up may be baited with enticements or propelled by tensions that take us in disturbing directions. Every aspect of the picture is a potential hook to hold us. We may be taken by the attractiveness of the cast, how good things are to look at, or how well they are presented, and our thought about what might happen may exert its tug. Characters and conflict are the stuff of storytelling, and people that we enjoy watching will contribute. They keep us better tied to the screen during periods of calm, and added concerns for their welfare elevate anxiety when dangerous situations are entered. Even in the absence of anxiety, people will engage us in the activities we watch them pursue, and we may begin to assume new viewpoints. Good characters, including well-fashioned bad ones, can also introduce driving concerns independent of fright. We will always wish the best for those we like, and strong feelings about someone deserving to be rewarded or punished stimulate the desire to see injustice set right. Our concern with individuals, however, has its limits. We had best find no unusual heroes here. Terror begins with diminishment, and rare strengths should be saved for the assailant. Although we worry more about likable characters, when it comes down to the crunch, old alliances don't count for much, and any innocent character triggers the same experience. People are expendable, and so are conflicts that turn out to be red herrings. Once unhooked, however, we are quick to go for recastings of concerns. Before it all settles down to a singular disturbance with a few individuals, we may be strung along by bait-and-switch tactics in an unbroken succession of new offerings.

Many attractions can engage us, and threads of lesser conflicts will add more pull, but only lines of primal nature wholly determine our direction, holding fast even when we try to break free. Tugging and relaxing, tightening their grip while reeling us in, they always send that sense of growing helplessness on our way to being gutted and consumed, that protracted taking of our entirety. The required line is selfhood's dissolution and its primal extinction, and its strength will be determined by its own unique composition. Premise is of paramount importance. Ideally it is an instantly chilling conception, thoughts rarely realized that make us squirm at the very idea. Beyond just getting us into the theater, good concepts take us all the way. Dreadful ideas must be wonderfully pictured. A frightening premise on paper should stay there unless it plays out with a rich array of psychic imagery. Even a story so good that it must be told must have its players tell the tale with compelling primal signatures.

Premises may employ forces we fear in everyday life, such as the surprisingly common belief in spirits or alien encounters. When combined with a concocted aura of actuality, this can go a long way for a more susceptible audience. Belief helped override defects in *The Exorcist*, saved *The Amityville Horror* (U.S.A., 1979) from a short run, and added more anxiety to *The Blair Witch Project* (U.S.A., 1999). Belief helps, but organic strength is in the pure and pictorial nature of the primal line.

Along with the one always there, four optional lines may be employed to reinforce tensions. *Unnaturalism* is one. Although horrific chillers are always an abnormal state of affairs, so deeply primal that they trigger the irrational, an unusually frightening premise may permit the surreal to be out in the open. Validating our worst fears, it justifies the display of nightmarish forces, altered imagery, and warped sound. And anything obsessed with having all of us is awesomely enhanced with more chilling possibilities.

Another useful selection is *totalism.* Just as the most terrifying menace is totalistic in nature and the most powerful photography is undiluted by nonessentials, horrific absoluteness may be completed by the line of action. We come to feel that every outside force is acting against us in some unnatural conspiracy. And when everything exists in a contained universe, a farmhouse, a spaceship, or even an isolated town small enough to be well known and visualized, having all of us can come to mean everyone.

A sense of *mystery* may also be useful. Concern with the unexplained enhances core experience in three ways. By our active involvement in thought, the investment of ourselves in seeking solutions, we become more personally connected to developing matters. Missing key information or the right connections, we also become the writer of worst-case scenarios and worry about all the alternative endings that we might have to face. Finally, and most importantly in times of anxiety, lack of normal understanding is terribly disturbing.

For films with few confrontations and much time to think, mystery is a valuable line of connection. Even minor mysteries void of anxiety are helpful. Why people or circumstances are the way they are may be made more intriguing by withholding some background until later, and some things are best left unsaid when we can come to understandings on our own. Major mysteries are inherently disturbing, and they usually involve identifying the enemy or its true nature. Good puzzles mislead us from what should be in plain sight. They also steer understandings to frightening false alarms and, far worse, a false sense of security. Similar to a good shocking sequence, the best mysteries will help viewers put things together in the best way to dismantle them. Already more unnerved by new disclosures, by imagery or insight we suddenly see it, and the revelation is worse than not knowing.

Surprise is a potential part of mystery, but it may also arrive with no more unknowns than what awaits us. The unexpected is the remaining line that may add power to the main one, and it is the only one applicable to every chiller. Unpredictability makes any movie more interesting, and for fright films it delivers blows that would have been softened by seeing them coming. Setup surprises are the most unsettling. Our anxiety is already elevated, and the discovery is invested with all that led up to it. The best are not so surprising upon review. Understandings suddenly come together in an unforeseen picture, one that will also be seen as entirely inevitable. Being formulistic and plentiful, chillers make the unexpected more difficult to fashion. Common standards and practices, however, create their own opportunities.

Strong screenplays build from expectations, employing conventions for anticipation and invention for surprise. Avoiding the obvious as well as the next one or two possibilities, the best scripts stay at least one step ahead of good second-guessing.

Although some uncertainty contributes to suspense and shock, there is no profit from blind confusion. Unfathomable chaos might be thought to be most frightening, but it will not work out that way. Meaningful measurements must always be made. When an invincible enemy absorbs every blow until one sends it senseless, when it may spring back to life, even repeatedly metamorphose with a whole new bag of tricks, the monster creates battles of surprising boredom. Even when you believe it, constantly changing the rules on us produces an uncertainty that undercuts anxiety. It is the same for some chase scenes that lose us, such as ones through hallways or thick woods where we separately see two people running but have no way to know their proximity. Our equated state requires basic information. Present confusion is best with a variety of clear judgments, and surprise will be strongest with some preparation.

Sounds of Alarm

Sound shapes what we see. Through our ears and neurological pathways that independently add their own emotions, we perceive the primal nature of assault. Coloring the tonality of mood and impression of imagery, sound may wholly transform the picture. It is an important part of shock, especially powerful when we have been made ready. With anxiety well primed, panic is best jump-started by a startling sound. Ideally it comes with a jolt of imagery, is created by what we see, and becomes part of the image's imprint. This essential startle response is diminished by films with too many loud disruptions, and it is undercut by the bad habit of adding artificial bursts of noise to false alarms.

For the most part, however, sound is an artistic choice and directorial decision, one allowing much freedom. It may punch up the tension by giving advance warning or be kept silent for shocking surprise. It should always amplify what is shown, but sometimes by adding other suggestions. Music may set the tempo of anxiety and form of emotion, and, more than just an atmospheric overture for danger, it can resonate the menace's inborn nature and present disposition, as well as the sense of our own disarray. The same can be said for all of the sound design. Despite so many alternatives, there is no doubt about the goal. The aim is the same as photography's, the realization of key perspectives. Surely for surreal or unnaturally primitive encounters, and even when they are superficially ordinary, sound should echo tremors of the primal presentation.

The introduction of digital technology, multitrack surround sound, clean and accurate from the faintest noise to seat-shaking explosions, has encouraged the overuse of its new capabilities. Silences are rare, and often anything that possibly could be heard stands out with unnatural clarity. Big battles in outer space or on our streets may profit from cacophony, and even their calmer moments might be made more immediate by the sharp reports of every sound, but more restraint pays off for chillers. Here the nature of alarm is deeper. Simple sounds have power to cut to the core and may carry a wide range of emotions, and most perform well even at low volume. Some are heard solo, inherently unnerving without perceived origin, while others come in concert with what we see, adding their own emotions to it. Especially with music, sound's rapid pulse may set the timing of our heartbeat, while, quite independently, having all of its other impressions create a picture that justifies such palpitations.

In a rural setting of well-separated houses, the night stalker has struck again. An old man has found what was left of his wife, and he is rushing for help through the gloom of a gathering storm. The wind is enlivened with unsettling emotion, approaching with a swelling moan of deep despair before sweeping the scene with a chilling howl and flight of fallen leaves. Dwarfed by a tall, denuded tree, grasped by the sway of bent branches, the old church is in sight. The bell begins to sound, and it might reduce our anxiety by hints of a helpful presence, but the strange pulsation of its resonance, the warping pitch and wavering strength, takes its toll on our senses with an eerie uneasiness. Inside, only to find the preacher hanged, bobbing up and down on the bell rope, we hear the bell fall silent, joining the quiet of the unlit room. The old man is frozen in fright when extended flashes of lightning provide a long view of empty space that matches the complete silence, and the sight is followed by a return to darkness before the low rumble of distant thunder.

Suddenly it is the wind again, this time hurling pellets of rain against the windows, and the tap, tap, tapping of a tree branch, its agitated insistence becoming increasingly hard to dismiss. The lightning's second strike comes with the briefly illuminated presence of the madman and a startling blast of overhead thunder. After a frenzied struggle and lucky escape, the exhausted old man hopes to have secreted himself in the bell tower. Sounds from outside are almost gone, but despite attempts to muffle himself, his heavy breathing is unending and alarmingly distinct. Its quickened pace is soon to include the terrifying counterpoint of a slow beat, the sure and steady, unrelenting footsteps coming up the staircase, the creak of old wood suggesting neither hurry nor attempt at concealment. Finally the stalker is at the top, and he slowly surveys the space with a murmuring expiration of breath that has the hint of a purr. An assault will end with the victim's head slammed against the bell with tremendous force, but we hear no gong or thud, just that awful, unmistakable crunching crack of collapsing skull before the face deflates of all expression.

When sound causes what we see to be stunningly graphic or makes only imagined suggestions perfectly clear, when it adds animalistic tones to a human assailant or gives human voice to forces of nature, or when it introduces an eerie unnaturalism to our everyday environment or simply finds disconcerting qualities within ordinary noises, its powerful impressions reshape our sense of circumstances. More than photography that is expected to render everything with the same resolution, sound portraits may be impressionistic and abstract. We do not notice if some sounds are absent, find it unacceptable if others are elevated or altered in character, or even wonder where the musical accompaniment is coming from. This form of reproduction is more akin to painting that may bring striking detail to significant areas while letting the rest fall away, and by adding layers of its own evocative texture. Similar to visual style, the chiller's best sound tracks are usually sparse, a highly selective orchestration of stirring effects with accentuation of essentials. Often the most alarming sound is silence, an emptiness with highly unsettling overtones, a stillness that also amplifies any shocking disruption. Invaluable for augmenting a threat's actual nature and psychic character, when surrounding us, sound will even become part of the picture's shape and size.

Dominant Size

Size matters. The magnitude of emotion reflects the picture's expanse and scope of sound. We feel the effect even from television. No matter how compelling the story or how much we try to put ourselves in the picture, watching a drama on a tiny portable pales in comparison with seeing it displayed on no more than an average-size set. Adding side speakers expands the impression of surrounding experience, and even action that might not have held our attention may become somewhat engrossing. Imagery commanding more of our field of view, especially when widened by sound, places us in the midst, and it adds import and urgency that is harder to dismiss. Encompassing visual and auditory space also helps to eclipse our actual setting. Sights and sounds outside of the presentation can soften experience to a surprising degree. They may not seem to be distracting, but their pernicious power will be illuminated by completely darkening and silencing the room. The bigger screen or moving closer helps make the picture more dominant and all else peripheral. There is more to size, however, than sensory envelopment and loss of diluting impressions. Actual size has inherent strength, and it is most felt at the movies. Viewing a film by gigantic projection is not the same as sitting close in a small theater or right in front of a home movie screen. They may make an identical imprint on our retina, but not our psyche. An evaluation of true magnitude amplifies its message. Enlarged exhibition is the best way to realize expansive subjects of horizontal sweep or towering scale, but there is an effect separate from realism. In horrific chillers, an oversize display of sign stimuli and psychic symbols triggers an unnatural inflation of reflexive reactions. Television, with the exception of the larger home-theater screens, so enormously underplays primal presentations that we may be left unchanged, and we are sure to be shortchanged when paying full price at undersize cineplexes.

The Power of Presentation

Good movies are composed of many qualities. They can take us to new places, deliver on the promise of an intriguing premise, present fully rounded characters and situations, exhibit fine craftsmanship in all departments, and display originality and intelligence. Some fright fans may even seek subtext. Seeing individuality being stripped by society or society being threatened as a whole, they may feel that sights meant to shock can also hide metaphor. Seeking less cerebral stimulation from vampire movies, that coupling swoon of complete surrender or sisterhoods of seductive bodies, languid, lost in trance, some viewers may find that these sights secrete sensual pleasures. We may have our own list of interests or share common standards while differing widely on priorities. Chillers should aim for every element of excellence, and any area of improvement is likely to strengthen the entirety. Compared with most narratives, however, far fewer factors figure into our overriding reactions, and we all agree on what they are. Our quality time is spent where the world is far simpler, a primal arrangement of just a few universals with fixed responses. Viewed within the restricted scope of a like-minded audience, good movies that leave us shaken may have a limited composition. Defined by emotion and measured by depth of experience, horrific chillers stand or fall on sensation. The best examples may excel in only a few areas, and these will be individually crafted to shared standards. This is where presentation can make the same story stronger or spin additional threads in the universal yarn.

The right sounds have horrific potential, and there will be moments when they are as important as imagery. Hooks are even more helpful. Confrontations take us completely, while an array of attractions keeps us headed down the garden path. The ones we like the most usually are the characters and their performers, and they make many contributions. Attachments to people may keep us watching, engage us in activities that assume their own life, connect us to human needs and desires, alter our perspectives, and add to anxiety when danger is indicated.

A well-mounted remake, *Invasion of the Body Snatchers* (U.S.A., 1978) brought high production values and other qualities of good moviemaking to a similar story, and more rounded characters were well performed. Our heightened interest in individuals allows a longer period to set up the situation that will come to hold us on its own. Any expectation, however, that more built-up connections would heighten the horror turns out to be unfounded. We may be a bit more nervous beforehand or unhappier after people are lost, but when terror takes over, these fully fledged friends might just as well be complete strangers. If there was any hope that polished color photography would be more effective than the low-budget black-and-white original, we are again disappointed. Although the new envisioning of developing replication was powerfully realized, production values were a poor trade for monochromatic bare essentials. Primal vision is always central to emotion, and it is here that a fundamental miscalculation was made in the screenplay. The notion of complete loss of selfhood spreading from everyone to us is as good as it gets for horrific totalism, and the remake replaces an isolated small town with a bustling big city. It was only logical that this would create even more opportunity for awesome envelopment, but being only logical is sure to miss emotion. Instead of a simple, closed space, a community that we feel we know well, we are in an expanse too busy with anonymous individuals and unseen livelihoods, far too big and complex to take it all in. Widespread destruction of the world's population is a more frightening thought, but primal perceptions are better set to see a small population in a circumscribed space, and there is heightened concern when each individual loss clearly diminishes the whole. Giving up tight containment and a sense of whole place for an expanded territory, the film quite predictably lost valuable ground. With all of its improvements, the remake is not as good as the original. The primal picture proves to be more important than overall depth and polish.

In addition to totalism, so well worked by body snatchers, lines of unnaturalism, mystery, or surprise may add their own tension to the one that must be used. These optional extras may be employed independently or in disturbing combinations. Entwining the supernatural with mystery turns a whodunit into a more unsettling what-is-it. Weaving totalism with surprise may allow for the awful discovery that everyone else is actually one of them. The tremble of working lines may be no more than red herrings, such as the supernatural's eerie sensations being felt from what will prove to have a far more ordinary explanation. Although these additions widen emotion and deepen connections, the greatest source of potential power is in the rendering of elements always there. Exceptional craftsmanship in two areas will significantly strengthen the singular formula. Most important is organic construction and timing. Sequences as well as entire films providing the complete experience are serial constructions of the same steps with similar elements, and the most frightening will always excel in the pacing and power of their engineering. The visualization of key perspectives is also essential for making the most of what we see. Here, too, good films follow many definable rules, the best finding new renderings of an unchanging picture. More important than plot, construction and visualization will always be the essence of strong presentation.

The best-made chillers need no anxiety to hold us, and they create mood and tension in between the defining periods of dreadful fright. Every component of good movies becomes more critical when the drama starts slowly, spaces key scenes with more ordinary events, or requires subtle reshaping of how things are seen. For most examples, however, fine overall qualities have diminishing returns, although it is certainly crucial to avoid mistakes. Turnoffs weaken ties to the entire picture. Silly situations, annoying characters and performers, or fakery of effects may destroy what was well done. We may be separated from the screen by a succession of phony or familiar false alarms, curiosity killed by cats in kitchen shelves. Audiences may give a free pass to a dubious premise even if it comes with the coincidence that some expert is handy, but other unlikelihoods risk having us call everything into question. Unless natural connections are broken, however, we respond reflexively to close-quarter confrontations, especially when they are horrifically primal, and everything outside of this exhibition becomes far less relevant. The surrounding narrative must achieve minimal standards, higher for some viewers than others, but once met, making it better may significantly improve the movie without adding much fear. The cover story of surface interests and secondary concerns is the delivery system for what we came for, that far simpler formula of insidious ingredients. As willing victims, seeking intoxication from escapist experience, we are forgiving of what gets us there, especially when under the influence.

Power arrives from the primal presentation. It may be all formula, but rules for its recipe take you only so far. For any production the special abilities of the correct people will pay off, and the genre would profit from their employment. It would begin with producers who have a better appreciation for the screenplay, who judge a project not only by the commercial pull of its premise and players, but by how well it is pictured and plays out on the pages. Most certainly, it requires writers with dark vision and the skill to flesh out the formula with new life of its own. Sensitivity to the same viewpoint should guide the selection of other key people. Not every good film-maker is equally adept. Cinematographers who always make it so real could expose shortcomings here. The editor who helped shape the last blockbuster might not quite cut it, offering less than the one with the pacing to save that comedy. Even successful directors of action and assaults might not be good choices. The best ones here can rivet our attention when not much is happening, and they have a keen sense of malignant forces far deeper than physical danger or mass destruction. Everyone in on the making of emotion should share the darker designs in the story's vision. Frightful expression in film, its bold strokes and subtle shadings, calls for a collaboration of conjoined artists.

XIV. Primal Orders

Horrific chillers are known by their sensations, a sense of something more than any ordinary danger or assault. Suspense overtakes us with intangible dread, and shock will strike with haunting impressions. Many diverse films of similar emotions were dissected, and all active ingredients came together with shared dimensions. The chiller's dark disorder revealed remarkable regularities, features found in every good example as well as every part of their construction. Whether it is individual scenes or overall themes, or the shape of circumstances, victims, or assailants, any part inspected will expose the same picture. It is a twofold assault upon selfhood: self's dissolution and primal extinction. Should there be any doubt, it will be boldly spelled out by the agent in three nonverbal languages with vocabularies of automatic meaning and emotion. Even when the film seems to be about something else—best described by another category—the most terrifying dramas are also monster movies. Danger may take the form of human beings, animals, forces of nature, or even normally non-living objects, but it will always be something animated with the same unnatural desires and visual signatures. In fact, everything that makes these movies has the same designs, and a simple equation of altered states factors our condition at each point in the picture. Expressing the strength and character of anxiety, it fits all forms of forced tension. We are subject to directives that may work over and over without awareness or against our will—irresistible orders that will assume a more telling order in a review of all our findings.

Circles of Consumption

Feeling our way through darkness, a night fog so thick that our outstretched arm is absorbed by the enveloping gloom, we find ourselves alone in an unfamiliar place. Moving ever so slowly, seeking signs of anything out there, we discover only emptiness and silence. Still probing the dark with arms held out, our unseen hand strikes something. We pull back and freeze. A short pause, then emerging from the vapor

---

right in front of us, standing frozen at the sharp edge of its shadow curtain, like a sunken corpse, cold and clammy, suddenly popping to the surface, is an awful sight. Its wet, gray skin is streaked with salt and what once was someone's face is now swollen with features washed away. Other than dark, empty sockets staring right at us, it shows no reaction to our presence or gasp of fright. Perhaps it cannot sense us. After a moment's wait, the thing appears about to speak, but then about the mouth, the bloated rot of flesh begins to sag, and suddenly the jaw falls away with a dreadful scream, a desperate cry turning guttural, lost in a deep, gurgling, last gasp for breath.

Whether we are in a crowded theater or all alone deep within ourselves asleep, there is no more awful place to be. Right here or somewhere similar is where we wind up in any worthwhile horror film. In all these movies we enter an environment with a center of terrible disturbance, a commotion encircled by shock waves sent rippling through the landscape. Diminishing with their distance from the core, every setting resonates tremors of engulfment.

The force is from a horrific being, its epicenter a spot inside the face. A dark cavity of consumption encircled by sharp teeth echoes the whole experience, the shredding of selfhood and its complete disappearance. The spot is encompassed by lips likely to twist a warning snarl with perverse contempt, and all of this is surrounded by a face barren of humanity, an emptiness filled with the ferment of single-minded assault. We see human malice coming with a delight and animal aggression unhinged. Unlike normally expressed warnings that keep us on our toes, these unnatural revisions trip us up, leave us off-balance, unsupported by a correct response. The face is its identity, an overlay of instinctual, learned, and symbolic imagery, all shared triggers of sure emotion. When its eyes are locked on us, insidious communications resonate their aim. Coming from the nice-looking children known to have alien ancestry in *Village of the Damned* (Great Britain, 1960), no more than the same sullen and superior, ice-cold stare cloned across their faces is terribly chilling, and our fear is not for the little ones. Expressions need not be extreme or features all that unusual for signatures to get under our skin with sensations of dreadful diminishment.

Stepping back a bit, we confront the whole being, a body shaped by the same dimensions and able to hold us in its embrace. Immediately in reach of the embodiment is the second circle of shock, and it heightens any assault. Even weapons, including primal ones, are weakened when leaving this area. The handheld blade, its dreadful swing or sudden thrust, its slow insertion or violent yank upward through the belly, or no more than the quick tweak to Nicholson's nostril by the creepy little twerp in Polanski's *Chinatown*—the gesture is empowered by being part of the assailant and the messenger of its individual emotions. Much is lost when the instrument is disconnected, hurled at a distant victim, or activated by psychic powers. Direct physical or mental contact with the being is far more frightening than anything it might throw our way.

The next circle is beyond reach, temporarily at a safe distance, but where we continue to experience unsettling proximity. Even if a horrific threat appears to be completely inactive, and there is enough running room should we need it, staying nearby is unusually disturbing.

Retreating to where facial features may have shrunk from sight, to a setting of more security, we are still struck by the menace's size and primal posture. It may be a body swelled and looming upward, limbs outstretched with all signs of threat deployed, or some portion of this picture. The inflation need not match our size. Something small suddenly enlarged may be a frightful sight of surprising magnitude. When naturally enormous, such as a spaceship, its impact can be awesome. Seen dead-on and coming straight at us, objects may assume life. Inborn images of alarm will be reviewed by a psyche set to seek out symbolic signs of pursuit, and horrific aims upon us may be felt even from nonliving matter. Should its motion be unnaturally slowed, retarded but still coming, dreadful sensations of relentlessness confirm the certainty of arrival.

The two least unsettling circles are beyond sight of the danger, but places where we still feel some trembles radiating from the epicenter. Marked by signs of its central inhabitant, the inner circle remains capable of delivering jolting shocks. Before-and-after images may strike us without warning. It could be the after-picture of danger's presence, the awful destruction left behind. It could come to include forewarnings, overtures of arrival, sounds that picture an awesome approach. In *Jurassic Park*, seated without concern inside a vehicle, we hear the loud resound of distant thuds, sounds similar to the muffled thumps of far-off cannon fire. Uncertainty is suddenly erased when shock waves resonate within cups of water on the dashboard, and we are instantly aware that even the earth is shaking with an annihilator's stunning approach. Without seeing the enemy, before-and-after images take us to confrontation. By so simply telling the story to our senses, they put us right on the spot with a shock of recognition. Pure and graphic primal imprints impress us with the shape and power of assault and with the fragility of ourselves.

Beyond the border of direct evidence, the outermost circle sends a few agitations and shivers. The setting will find a way to fashion impressions of its core. We are still within the creature's world, an environment shaped to the same ends. Even if introducing no danger of its own, it may isolate, disorient, inhibit movement, alter our boundaries, and symbolically suggest a setting of destruction. Both physically and by imagery, it stands ready to separate us from ourselves.

Levels of Loss

The other side of where we find ourselves is how we stand. Lost and alone in night fog, even seeing part of us disappear, all sight and sense of place taken away, we are suddenly unable to act or understand as we confront a decomposing stranger. Already diminished, we look down to see our withdrawn hand shriveled up, dripping wet, and losing color. Soon we are all awash, our drenched skin turning milky white, wrinkling in some places while puffing up in others, softening and eroding all of the features in our face. There is the horrible realization that this monster from the mist is not an enemy. It is some nameless victim of the vapor, an awful specter of what soon will be us.

The position that we see assumed is where we find our own experience. The victim may see things differently, feel himself to be in a far better or even worse position, but our feelings are from a separate perspective. Measured by their strength and importance, proximate forces are seen to create reduced standing. In chillers this reduction is sure to be the essence of self. Primal signatures in the setting and its center now also mark our position, striking us with dreadful diminishment.

A heroic protagonist with unusual assets may not provide the experience until he has been cut down to size, even if he was outmatched from the start. It all begins to count when we stand reduced of normal abilities. Minor breakdowns or simply a submissive posture may be felt beyond logical outcomes. Handicaps, even if temporary, may make a lesser peril more disturbing than a more likely danger faced with full faculties and commanding attitude. Perfect victims are the young or elderly, infirm or handicapped in sight, mobility, or mental functions, fragile females, or anyone not equal to what we feel to be our normal selves. The lack of awareness of proximate danger also displays primal disablement. Even if these deficits should make no impact upon outcome, they still carry a fearsome feeling of incompleteness. Loss of personal firepower is more upsetting than the loss of a weapon, more frightening than an equivalent gain in the opposition, and the nature of sensation is far more troubling.

Similar to the circles where we stand, forms of loss may be ordered by primal alarm. Simply seeing someone impeded from nonessential pursuits provides some anxiety, and the feeling will heighten with peril. Chillers introduce themselves at a deeper level where those lacking togetherness face indications of danger, and organic stress becomes psychic fright. Personal boundaries dissolve in a setting of unnatural isolation and invasion. Lost awareness, understandings, or any ordinary capability will deepen dread. Horror arrives in the face of the enemy, a reduction by physical and psychic threat. Diminishment is complete when the threat is realized, and the loss of our most identifying features is most disturbing. Especially in the face, disfigurement by injury, decomposition, or any surgical or surreal transformation is dreadful, and even worse when we see the slow process of our dissolution on its way to extinction. The darkest and deepest level lies beyond loss of life. It may take us to a living state of erased identity, left alive, yet stripped of memories and personal features, where even madness might be better than no mind at all.

Depth of Delivery

Any event may be presented in various manners, portrayals that differ in depth of their transmission. Some, with differing levels of emotion, give us all the information without the experience. Others dig deep inside to our very core. Within the structure of most films, a well-told tale is better than a visual flashback, keeping pictures for the present while bringing up the past with only imagined imagery. For our complete inclusion, however, no thousand words are worth a picture.

A described event may sound to be frightening, even create some anxiety, but it is not happening to us. Cold facts provide the shallowest communication. Words imparting more than knowledge go a bit deeper. The reporter's inflection may provide mood, his timing create suspense, and his language evoke pictures. A villain's selection of words, emotions suggested or even their absence, can also sharpen the portrait of what we see, and brand-new concerns are nicely started by just a few choice words and tone of voice. Bad tidings by way of sound are more powerful. Similar to imagery, a sound's imprint is direct, not fabricated from thought, and it resonates with emotion. Startling jolts leave us badly shaken, and even subtle sound prints may be deeply troubling. Impressions may forward a picture of what will be coming or completely alter what is right in front of us.

The delivery is deeper when the threat is seen, and more so when elements of its imagery add their own emotion. To feel the press of circumstances, however, we must see both sides, and see them in close confrontation. Should the sight also include primal signatures, delivery will reach the darkest depths.

Once experienced, conflict may be activated by communications too shallow to take us on their own. Sounds associated with earlier upheavals could take us back to where we were before. A word or two could disclose a terrible twist, some ghastly notion that, even without adding any danger, chillingly changes the whole fabric of the situation—or it could be something said by a trusted character that creates the shocking realization that he is on the other side. Although many revelations may be effectively presented in verbal terms, words will always be more disturbing when coming with the imagery and expressive tone of a deeper delivery.

In Hitchcock's delightful and gripping *The Thirty-Nine Steps* (Great Britain, 1935), a desperate protagonist gives himself up to a stranger, a man he believes will shield him from authorities and keep a state secret from getting into the hands of a foreign agent, someone known only by a missing little finger. When asked if he knows which hand, our friend suggests the left, but a follow-up question requires no answer. Raising his right hand with the lost finger, the stranger casually inquires if this could be the one. Now all is lost, and it is all the more shocking due to its startling imagery and the indifferent, offhanded manner in which the missing finger is held up to our eyes. Cold facts are sufficient to trigger earlier conflicts, but the power of past presentations will be compounded by the depth of their revival.

Primacy of pictures is seen everywhere. What we see is what we get, and what we only know can't hurt us. A man with murderous intent will not be frightening before he strikes unless he displays primal features. Creatures of horrific casting, if off somewhere unseen simply pulling the strings, reshape us only by what is seen. Ordinary-appearing people acting on satanic orders will not bring surreal sensations to their assault, and battles with armadas of flying saucers, despite their unearthly crew, will be experienced as any other high-tech war film. Unseen tragedies are escaped, and they count only to the degree that they alter the balance of viewed conflicts. On-screen suffering may make us unhappy, but we will not suffer the experience without seeing it happen. Figures and forces must be pictured and closely connected, and the force that we feel reflects the power of imagery and sound. The strongest images are concrete and elemental, graphically evocative with a minimum need of intellect. The most disturbing of these pictures go all the way with bold psychic signs of primal assault on both sides of the conflict.

Waves of Disturbance

During our passage through a fright film, we are struck by waves of anxiety—waves with a force that combines level of loss with depth of its delivery. Some serious forms of loss are not well visualized on-screen, and lesser ones that are more easily pictured will prove to be more disturbing. Internal problems, mental or medical issues that make it more difficult to rise to certain occasions, will make times of crisis more troubling. They are, however, less frightening than viewable diminishments or physical restraints, and they will not be experienced on their own. Even small external signatures of unseen deficits may make all the difference. A protagonist knows that his life is in danger but is unaware of a homing device inserted in his brain. Our knowledge of the implant will heighten our concern when he is being followed, but the sight of a tiny scar on his skull will disturb us at any point in the picture, and it will carry its own unsettling feeling.

Not all depictions of a similar loss strike us the same way, even when they are actively presented. We may witness a convincing enactment of brainwashing and feel the isolation and unrelenting intimidation. Lacking symbolic psychic signatures, however, the presentation will never assume an insidious suggestion of mind control within us. Should we see someone wake up in bed with aliens in the room, experience may be more profound and to the point. Two creatures restrain the horrified victim while a third approaches with long crablike appendages encircling a small spot of facial features. The arriving face comes to rest within inches of the victim's, then pulls back a bit, silently surveying the other with curiosity. Suddenly the larger claws dart forward, clamping hold of the man's head, immobilizing it for a moment before the slender right-and-left appendages begin to bore into both ears. The alien's lidless, slit eyes widen, and its tiny mouth drops open as the overcome individual remains wide awake while becoming completely impassive. The imagery of the embrace is at once hypnotic and horrifying, and we join the person in being overtaken by the dreadful sense of being erased and replaced that was escaped from the more credible and lengthy enactment of brainwashing.

Beyond making our experience of loss true to form, depth of delivery will be felt later. After being left in a seemingly normal state, both victims will be called upon to be in service to some conspiracy. The situation for the brainwashed character is made more disturbing due to his understood disability, but we are more anxious over what he might do than sharing a sense of his missing self. Circumstance for the one under alien control will feel worse. By the shape and strength of its creation, we personally continue to sense being wide open to outside directives.

Waves of disturbance follow fixed rules. They arise from the sight of any innocent figure facing threatening forces with fondness for people not figuring into it. Although one person's place is automatically computed, more in the same spot will barely be counted. We see the entire crew of a sailboat swept overboard and the craft sail on unmanned. While it may have been momentarily more shocking to see so many go at once, unless the mass of people approaches an awesome size, our disturbance soon settles to seeing no more than one. Agitations will be heightened simply by alternating in strength, the ebb and flow of turbulence being more unsettling than floundering in place. They will also be worse when we are provided a weaker position, such as a child or anyone unable to swim. Although added victims do not multiply one condition, distinctly different losses will be combined. Should someone in the water be out to do another one in, when we see their life-or-death confrontation while a child struggles to stay afloat, we acquire two states at the same time. Strung together through shifting forces, multiple exposures may change in character from moment to moment. This most easily occurs when more factors are included, especially when they are bipolar in nature. Enter a shark with its horrific signatures, a third threat that, if aimed at the villain, could also cut it back to two.

Include a small raft, large enough to save a few people, but also a potential source of strife, and the possible permutations become enormous. Struck from all sides by different waves of disturbance made more unsettling by moments of calm, caught up in crosscurrents of conflict and unforeseen undertows, losing all control within the rising swell, we see no help in sight and all sense of safe haven inside ourselves being swept away.

The Horrific Journey

Even a still picture will not remain motionless. Seen frozen in frame, the menace makes no move on its victim, but its hold strengthens while we watch by reinforcing connections. The scene may also rekindle earlier emotion or completely shift in character as symbolic thinking makes step-by-step discoveries. Movies are a rapid succession of moments that create continuous motion, their movement turning into developing stories. In chillers, these pictures frame our own standing, constantly shifting while taking a singular direction.

Our journey unfolds within a realm of primal conflict, a landscape laid out in closing circles of consumption, and each place will impress its shape on us. In repeated short excursions we pass from the outskirts, through the interior of its territory, to a confrontation at its core. Either by travel or by transformation of where we are, the setting shifts from circle to circle. It is the overall arc of the picture, and every defining sequence will cover the same ground.

Our most frightening times usually go the same way. Even upon entering we sense signals of what lies ahead, and the area's enveloping expanse or enclosure begins to erode our boundaries. Inside the next circle of more ominous surroundings, indicators of alarm more clearly shaped by primal signatures elevate anxiety. We may be struck by shocking evidence of a past presence or by disturbing signals of arrival. A yet to be seen enemy has dissolute emptiness and surreal possibilities, and our inability to give it shape adds to our own dissolution. We may be frightened by an advance warning, and then put in the spot of a blind victim. No preview, however, spares us the jolt of sight and sound when a sudden appearance confronts us. Now inside the circle of its presence, we experience more than momentary shock. Even beyond the enemy's grasp, we are within the reach of an aura that grabs hold of our insides. Looming large and set to strike, the destroyer reduces us with displays of its demeanor. The face is more horrific, an awesome assemblage of irresistible sensations and undefendable warnings. If flight is possible, it will be through a place that separates us from help and inhibits our defenses, a detour that turns out to take us through the deepening dissolution of ourselves.

We are headed for that face with its center consumption, and one way or another we will be dismantled or gone altogether.

The generic film as a whole follows its key sequences, taking the same course in the rape of identity, our capacity and completeness, and completing our passage from insignificance to the possible vanishing point. Our trip takes off, propelled by a few waves of disturbance, a swell arising from what we know about the premise and see in the setting of its circumstances. We may wish the best for our protagonist, and his survival will assume special significance if he is seen as someone able to help out, but our time is independent of lasting attachments. Direct participation is through serial and sometimes simultaneous states of many persons that often combine into uninterrupted periods of personal experience. Our journey of no return may be repeated, and separate excursions to the center will be taken as surges in a singular odyssey. It begins with a sense of separation from the world that we left and our viewpoints becoming conditioned to a place with its own perspectives. Our reorientation may come unexpectedly early on with a horrific flashback or fresh event, but it will soon settle back to the course of generic sequences. We are introduced to an unsettling place shaping our direction by bent of its design. At a loss in understanding and control, we are swept toward the interior by swells of disturbance, isolating emptiness and enveloping assault, two folded fronts of organic jeopardy with similar sensations. Periodically, from out of nowhere, huge waves will wholly overtake us, sweeping us up in a dissolution of all defenses and hurling us back down into the turmoil of primal extinction. There will be periods of calm, even times when we can reverse our direction, but prevailing forces will always take over. Sudden surges of compounding strength will propel us to a place too close to avoid a showdown. We are engulfed by the being's presence. Serially stripped of strengths and selfhood, separated from all support, facing unnaturally overpowering forces, and aimed at the most horrifying destruction, we are swamped by a dreadful realization of absolute helplessness. As a battered and lost last survivor, we are at the edge of the innermost circle, offered up to an abyss of consumption. An extended climax will conclude with us swallowed up into nothingness or left less than whole, still able to tell the tale.

While coming to see and understand danger more clearly, we do not simply sharpen its image. We confront distinctly different pictures of the same menace during the course of our journey. Its introduction may be a fast unfolding of developing snapshots, a flutter of primary features, a short assemblage of first impressions that includes what was missing with what was shown. Its unseen whole, an amorphous, barren void, is as much a feature as those graphically depicted, and it magnifies the importance of each feature that is seen along with its awful embodiment of emptiness. This is how we see it, for now a complete picture, a collage of real, symbolic, and merely imagined perceptions that will be its substance until the next sighting.

With new pieces of imagery and bits of information we will put new ones together, building embodiments increasingly horrific to our eyes. Part of their impressions is what they take from us, and we are sure to see more signs of our decomposition. We may even come to see the entity entirely differently with a ghastly revelation of its actual nature. Without doubt, it will take a final shape, seen and understood in its entirety, a stunning image that leaves no room for any other possibilities.

Dread should be ever present. It keeps us in the journey between big events and adds to their impact. With idling anxiety ready to go, good flights take off from a dread start. Although our peril feels to be far more than physical, a reversed roller coaster ride is the track of our emotion—some ups with more downs gaining in momentum, with the deepest descent saved for last. Even if we have experienced extinction earlier in the picture, we may continue to be taken deeper into the setting's dark interior. Encounters take different shape, compounding the forms of our loss. Presentations become longer, more complete, richer in evocative detail, and expose more primal signatures. New assaults gain power by being part of the same widening conflict, and all ongoing equations will be combined as we are taken to the end. Everything seems to be set for the same thing, separate circumstances in an unnatural alliance that assumes the totalism of the enemy. This expanding picture of closure and its aura of inevitability heads us helplessly toward our destination. If the developing context includes the film's whole population on its way to zero, we will feel an even more dreadful sense of closing consumption. When the number of people is reduced to one, a diminishing person now all alone, never more to know anyone, we best experience that terrible knowing of nothingness.

The trip may be more disturbing when taken in optional directions, paths introducing totalism, unnaturalism, mystery, or surprise. The experience is most expanded, however, by the artful crafting of essential ingredients. A fixed succession of stages sets the course of our emotions. From overall development to split-second timing, fine-tuning the flow of our conditions is critical. Cinematography, by its individual compositions and collective style, also shapes the story we see. The camera may not lie, but it easily adds its own impressions to the telling, and there are times that we may justifiably blame the messenger for the meaning and magnitude of bad news. Powerful realizations of key perspectives evoke surrealistic sensations and thought, enhance the enemy while diminishing the victim, and may enliven everything with an individualized aura of destruction.

In all the arts and crafts there is something to be said for simplicity. Pictorially it shows in the strength of an uncluttered composition, a frame filled by the power of just a few elements. In action it even adds to sequences of unfolding danger and destruction. More disturbing than an unending introduction of new forces is the reworking of what is in front of us. Change is more compelling when the same parts of the setting work for and against us in different ways or the same pieces of imagery express entirely new meanings. There is power in economy, and by carefully selecting key elements and keeping them all in play, everything may continually rearrange themselves into an array of more alarming conditions.

Altered Renderings

The degree to which films depart from the formula diminishes their impact. Even when horror is the main objective, not all good stories can contain every ingredient. Missing elements may be partially restored, but only by following strict primal rules.

Exhibiting obsession and totalism, the danger should assume a humanlike form, its vacant face, wiped away and awash with dissolution, is also full of dire warnings. Instantly on sight it strikes us with chilling sensations of its destructive means and motives, and in close confrontations its form will reshape us. Some plots do not allow for a complete reproduction of the being. Altering the portrait too far, however, reduces its power even when the menace is properly presented in striking situations. Horror is lost to the extent that the destroyer's appearance is overly like the rest of us or is insufficiently human. Nonliving forces or objects will work only when they may be visually anthropomorphized without seeming silly, and they will have to be fortified with obsessive intent and totalism. If too human in imagery, people lacking features of absent humanity, aberrant motives, or primitive assault, horror will also be missing. Here some signs should be provided during periods of stalking and striking, obsessiveness that dismantles our defenses followed by primitive assault that wholly disables us. Posture and choice of weapon can help, as can the camera's angle, lighting, selection of what is seen, or disturbing changes made by veil, fog, or altered reflection. When isolated features are seen in quick glimpses, they assume unusual power and complete a primal impression of an entire presence.

Any replacement too human or nonhuman in appearance must excel in reducing people and marking them with primal signatures. Once connected to terrible experiences, even ordinary appearing villains will assume some horror when stalking. This added air of alarm given to these stripped-down stand-ins, however, is far less dreadful than the aura that surrounds the most frightening people, an aura of invincible malevolence that remains ever present and resonates from every fiber of the being. The monster should be seen for what it is, and more than surface expressions and adopted postures, signals should be permanent parts, its inborn identity. Only a few signs suffice, and they need not be bold abnormalities when marking a commanding presence with bad behavior. Embodiments completed by context, however, must be fortified by fine performances. Coming with casting correctly sculptured faces and bodies is the need to employ actors who bring artful displays of what's inside. These under-players do not try to impress us with the familiar theatrics of dramatic acting. True performers, they become disturbing individuals who reveal singular interests within the complexities of human nature, people who even in everyday matters, by subtle signs or personal reactions, give chilling glimpses of how they fail to see the world the way we do. Along with some features of an unnatural predator made and motivated for its perverse profession, we should see an undeniably real person, impossible to dismiss.

Appearances count, but they aren't everything. Even the most horrific specter must maintain first impressions by living up to its looks. The failure to deliver on its promises takes a few forms. There are, of course, the obvious impostors. Even if aware of some artifice, we must take the creature most seriously, and unconvincing performances, confrontations, or even surroundings will strip it of power. Other imperfect reproductions have more subtle flaws. Monsters may remain frightening, but fall far short of their potential. Some assail people who one way or another are asking for it. Heroes are one example. We will side with someone out to kill, capture, or change the creature, but their choice in the matter and heightened posture lessens our reduction. Such situations must be altered, and the person's sudden loss or even death is insufficient. Bold achievers must become unwillingly trapped in a losing position and slowly stripped of choice and defenses before the confrontation concludes. For victims inviting assault, however, they are a far better selection than people deserving of punishment. Should the menace be acting out of a shared sense of injustice, our position in the encounter may be reversed. Heightening the victim's helplessness or making his demise more shocking does not help. Even cruel and unusual punishment will do no more than repel us with gruesome imagery. A victimized creature must move on to innocents who did nothing to hurt it and firmly establish its wholly nihilistic nature by assaulting them with even more relish.

It is also a mistake for a monster to employ agents that do not mirror its message. Fearsome-faced demons fail to follow through with us by merely assailing victims with flying objects, objects disconnected from their bodies, not frightening on their own, unable to consume willpower, or failing to perform primal extinction. Absent instigators are even more removed from the picture. A terrifying presence is lost when employing surrogates of wholly human appearance or when creating personal catastrophes by remote control, at best providing some eeriness to our thoughts when reflecting on the whole situation. It will help if the instigator has been seen attacking and now uses substitutes of similar form. Fully realized assault, however, arrives only with face-to-face confrontations, diminishment by direct touch of the enemy's physical or psychic power. Making an imperfect imprint of itself on others not only reduces anxiety but robs the experience of the creature's individual nature.

When films have few confrontations, little graphic violence, or threats short on primal signatures, context may enhance experience. More restrained envisionings must be formed slowly and artfully, conditioning our perspectives to the setting and to the viewpoints of others. Distinctive images will assume unusual significance when seen to share similar dimensions, and they should be portraits of the unseen danger, suggestive of its form and desires. They should also be developing pictures of ourselves. Inside a reshaped setting of unsettling possibilities, we may begin to assume similar shape, and even minor breakdowns of abilities will be unusually unnerving. A short, shocking sequence, even if impressionistically rendered rather than fully documented, will be especially disturbing and will color the rest of the picture. Slow construction of imagery and emotion proves useless, however, if the primal form does not appear and dominate. Impressions of conflict will begin to undermine rather than augment anxiety if expectations fail to be realized. Too much disturbance in the outer environment with too little pull from forces at its center leaves us floundering rather than feeling swept toward the abyss.

Excess is far more common than incompleteness, and the overuse of dream sequences is one example. Dreams are often employed to insert periods of terror with presentations not possible within the confines of the story, and they provide an opportunity to picture primal confrontations with all of the signatures. They are, however, an inefficient vehicle for evoking shared experience, and they are likely to become counterproductive. Someone awake may be assailed by hallucinations, and we will still participate. The forces may be imagined, but not the victim. Illusionary victims don't amount to much. What we know to be all a dream is seen at a safer distance, and, should we find that we have been fooled into thinking that it was real, the feeling that we have been unfairly alarmed may separate us from the film. Deadening our response to horrific action and imagery, these misdirected attempts to punch up the picture waste what should be saved for more effective deployment. Dreams may be shapers of shared experience, but they are not a good substitute. Avoiding overkill, they should be haunting omens, impressionistic previews that await real life to assume complete form and implication.

Excess is most likely with actual assaults. Horrific beings are best confined to a few appearances. Even instantly alarming features have a limited life, and, if their owner's repetitive behavior becomes routine, the power of first impressions starts to pale. Too much graphic slaughter also dulls our sensibilities, and too often it is a succession of similar assaults with little impact on the plot or our developing destruction. More of the same provides diminishing returns. The film should bring fresh situations, and with every visit the creature should come with something new, more of itself, such as an unseen feature, an added revelation about its origin or intent, or, at least, a stunning display of how easily it can come to get us. The most powerful enactments are not interchangeable replays of the same assault. They are changed by what came earlier, alter the future, take another part of us away, or add to the imagery that marks their meaning. They may remove someone most able to help others or, in a circumscribed setting, create the sense of totalistic consumption. When the worst is withheld until later, experience will continue to expand. Assaults should be cut back, conserving their limited resources. More powerful renderings of a person's slow dissolution reduce the need for so much extinction. Less will also be more disturbing when encounters make matters worse and deepen their aim on selfhood.

Orders of Unrest

This study gives some truisms an enthusiastic thumbs-up, while others receive mixed reviews. It is often stated that films are mostly a matter of imagery, and this proves to be remarkably so for the horrific chiller. The genre is regarded as being formulaic, and that turns out to be true beyond all expectations. The idea that these films reflect the fears of childhood is correct, but it misdirects our understanding of their origin. Given that we are activated by only a simple model of alarm shared with other animals, it is safe to assume that our response is rooted deep in our ancestry. It is also likely that concerns about boundaries within a consuming universe ruled by shapes of sensation begin with our earliest understandings in infancy.

The least accurate notions involve the nature of suspense and the role of our imagination. The dictionary definition of suspense—uncertainty and apprehension while awaiting an outcome—could be better refined for film. Some uncertainty may add to anxiety, but complete confusion does not compute, and we become most disturbed by shifting measurements. More important, anticipation is a minor matter. Dire possibilities are crucial, but our condition reflects what is now here. We may be waiting and wondering, but the press is from the present, the immediate imagery of an assault already in progress. It can be the unnerving inability to complete the picture of danger, or, when seeing someone unaware of approaching destruction, an intolerable impotence stripped of self-protection. Finding ourselves mired in a swamp along with a predator, it will be the ghastly sensation of personal paralysis, a feeling that may be worse than being overrun. Everything assumes the character of what we see. The seriousness of suggested outcomes adds its own level of urgency, but feelings follow the form of present perceptions, and unless we have taken the same trip earlier in the picture, our moment-by-moment sense of place in the journey bears little likeness to our anticipated destination.

For deep fright it is often stated that nothing matches the power of our free-roaming imagination. It is true that many films are more frightening while the danger remains amorphous, and they disappoint us with a clear definition. This still does not say that the unseen is more unnerving than the graphic depiction of a worst nightmare. It also begs the question whether our imagination is free at all. Even when possibilities appear to be wide open, we usually envision a given picture, private screenings in our mind's eye written and directed by the film in front of us. There is a place for this imagination, and another one for clarity, and they are the two periods in our passage. As we begin to lose ourselves, nothing equals the haunting power of partial perceptions fleshed out inside our heads. We have seen a surreal abstraction, an awesome entity of a few primal elements with an unnatural emptiness that is part of its picture. It is the image of dissolution, and our personal reduction by incomplete sight and understandings puts us in a similar state. In the end, however, the time for our removal, nothing can replace a completed, horribly detailed actualization.

The dominance of emotion over intellect is always facilitated by fear, and even surreal situations will be seen with more than a suspension of disbelief when we feel their forces deep within ourselves. Primal fear takes us to the dark domain of the chiller's experience. We are displaced to a spot with no middle ground or need for sophisticated understanding, a place where absolute evil is in opposition with helpless innocence, a setting with no room for sentiment, even from us. It is also a landscape of no ordinary imagery, where shapes are no more than assemblages of unsettling signals. We are where we all become alike, and the urgency of conditions makes all else of little consequence. Even if first recognized only by higher mental processes, the enactment will be instantly reduced to rudimentary understandings, and sensations of pure experience send terrifying statements with an immediacy and power that cannot be denied. We are also at the movies, helpless participants, completely stripped of all control. Throughout it all, all that counts in our condition is a simple assessment. Images of animalistic alarm are overlaid with human symbols of diminished selfhood, and instinctually driven organic anxiety is transformed by the dread of lost existence.

Not all of us are drawn to repulsion, but chillers are usually seen with more than informed consent. Thrills are eagerly awaited in an open invitation to escapist experience. During the course of the picture we will have to lose new friends, normally far from fun, but primal fright excludes all other feelings, nicely delivering the rush without the downer. There are, of course, differences between us that affect our reactions. People differ on standards required to hold their attention, and, even when those standards are met, we differ on susceptibility. Some of us, proven to be those most often given to daydreaming, become unusually absorbed in any dramatized presentation. Young people are also more likely to be good audiences. All of us, as we grow older, become better armed against the irrational, and we are all being steadily desensitized to pictured violence inside and outside theaters. Films often carry personal connotations and perspectives, especially their central subject matter. Some viewers are ready for supernatural assault, others respond more to everyday possibilities, and a few may encounter phobias. In short order, however, primal orders will take over, and, despite our differences, the hardened and the squeamish will respond to these alarms at levels set by their order of primacy. For each person, the equation will prove precise, predicting the relative power of their fright and the particular nature of its sensation.

We will know it when we see it and enter the picture. We will see imagery with designs on our psyche and terror in mind. In a world revealed by messengers of immediate emotion we witness the voiding of personal power and appearance, possibly to the point of disappearance. Sitting in a darkened theater, struck by shadows on a screen, we will find ourselves unassembled, disarmed, and consumed.

Plates

1. Lon Chaney as the new tenant of the Balfour estate; *photographer* Merritt Gerstad.
   London After Midnight   1927   b&w   MGM

2. Max Schreck as Nosferatu/Count Orlok; *photographer* Fritz Arno Wagner.
   Nosferatu   1921   b&w   Prana Films

3. Lon Chaney as Eric the Phantom; *photographer* Charles Van Enger.
   The Phantom of the Opera   1925   b&w   Universal

4. Vincent Price as Professor Henry Jarod in pursuit of Sue Allen (Phyllis Kirk);
   photographer Bert Glennon.
   House of Wax   1953   color/3-D   Warner

5. Max Schreck as Nosferatu watching Ellen; *photographer* Fritz Arno Wagner.
   Nosferatu   1921   b&w   Prana Films

6. Bella Lagosi as Count Dracula; *photographer* Karl Freund.
   Dracula   1931   b&w   Universal

7. Boris Karlof as the monster confronting Dr. Henry Frankenstein (Colin Clive);
   photographer Arthur Edison.
   Frankenstein   1931   b&w   Universal

8. Max Schreck as Nosferatu disappearing; *photographer* Fritz Arno Wagner.
   Nosferatu   1921   b&w   Prana Films

Dust jacket (front and back) ***Nosferatu***; *photographer* Fritz Arno Wagner.

Gallery and jacket design by Lonnie Duka.

Note (on not having any)

Starting with no footnotes, we are left with no appendix or bibliography. If I had to abandon my own preconceptions, I certainly was not about to listen to anybody else's. I went in blind, not even knowing how to start, simply to see with assurance what we all see for sure. Avoiding some terminology of arts and sciences, and any lingo with loose meanings that pass for understandings, I attempted independent description. This was not to be an encyclopedia of horrific films or a compendium of wide-ranging, hard-to-pin-down or prove opinions. Proven elements of every viewer's experience was the only subject, no more than sure observations and clear conclusions.

D.A.

Framing the Dark

Typeset and printed by Puritan Press, Inc., Hollis, NH.
Bound by Acme Bookbinding, Charlestown, MA.

Composed in New Baskerville, designed by John Baskerville, 1757.
Sprocket designed by Bitstream, Inc.
Plates are quadratones.

Thanks to copy-editors Michael Trotman and Emily Crehan for their good catches and thoughtful suggestions; and to Puritan Press, Inc., especially Don Trageser, for their fine work and additions to my page design. D.A.